JANET MITCHELL

Photograph by Douglas Macrae

JANET MITCHELL, LLD. HON. U. OF C., R.C.A., C.S.P.W.C., A.S.A.

JANET MITCHELL

Life and Art

PEGGY ARMSTRONG

1990

Hyperion Press Limited extends thanks to Masters Gallery Ltd., the Alberta Foundation for the Literary Arts, the Manitoba Arts Council, and Canada Council for their support.

ISBN 0-920534-87-2; 0-920534-91-0 (leather)

Designed by A. O. Osen
Typeset by Raeber Graphics Inc.
Separations by GB Graphics
Printed by Premier Printing Ltd.

Canadian Cataloguing in Publication Data

Armstrong, Peggy, 1941-
Janet Mitchell: life and art

Includes bibliographical references.
ISBN 0-920534-87-2; 0-920534-91-0 (leather)

1. Mitchell, Janet, 1912-. 2. Painters — Canada — Biography. 3. Women painters — Canada — Biography. I. Mitchell, Janet, 1912-. II. Title.

ND249.M57A93 1990 759.11 C90-097161-4

PRINTED IN CANADA

To J.C.A.

ACKNOWLEDGMENTS

I have been fortunate to have had some very special people helping me with this book.

At the top of the list is the artist herself, *Dr. Janet Mitchell,* whose life and art are rich sources of inspiration. I thank her for her gift of time and friendship.

Rod Green of Masters Gallery Ltd. in Calgary has provided invaluable assistance as well. I thank him for his financial support, his continual encouragement, and his knowledgable advice. Without him the completion of this project would have been infinitely more difficult.

I wish to thank *The Alberta Foundation for the Literary Arts* who played a significant part in this work in terms of both finances and morale through its generous, unconditional support of an older "new" writer.

John Snow of Calgary has applied his impressive skills as a master printmaker to complete Dr. Mitchell's limited edition prints included with the Collector's Edition of this book. I thank him for his significant contribution to this project.

Joan Murray's preface has added an important dimension by placing the work of Janet Mitchell within the larger context of Canadian art. *John Dean,* of John Dean Photographs Inc. in Calgary, has photographed 36 of the paintings reproduced in this book. And *Michael Lavoie* and his blue pencil helped me to cut a clear path through a complex project at a formative stage. I thank them all for their expertise and their generous donation of time and attention.

Finally, I would like to thank all the owners of Mitchell works who allowed me to reproduce their paintings in this book. My association with them led me to a better understanding of the remarkable power of communication that Janet Mitchell's art has with its audience.

CONTENTS

PREFACE

JANET MITCHELL *Celebrating Life* —— During a career spanning five decades, Janet Mitchell has transformed herself from a Western watercolorist into a maker of joyous, figurative pictures which veer at times toward the semi-abstract — her images, floating in soft radiant colors, evoke strongly the idea of the oneness of all life forms. This book demonstrates that despite these shifts of gear, Mitchell has all these years been very much the same woman, addressing her problems courageously, independently, and with increasing eloquence.

Mitchell's gems are her watercolors which, if they lack the scale of some of her large paintings, have an intimacy and charm. They reveal the artist's intuitive way of constructing a composition — often she lets the colors flow randomly to form the design until they arrive at something improbably, though hectically, alive. Mitchell uses chance as a pictorial element so the completed work has a way of shifting before the viewer's eyes. It is this quality that joins her to three other artists, her friend Marion Nicoll and two members of the Painters Eleven, Alexandra Luke and Jock Macdonald. Both Nicoll and Luke were inspired by Macdonald to probe nature and express the unexplored regions of the mind. Macdonald in turn had been inspired by Grace Pailthorpe, an artist with links with the British surrealist movement. Pailthorpe introduced Macdonald to automatism in 1943, and he did further research based on André Breton's automatic writing technique. He told Nicoll about it in 1946. She had already heard of the Quebec *Automatistes* through *Canadian Art* magazine but what Macdonald told her whetted her appetite. "Sit quietly, and let your hand write by itself on a page," he said. He meant for her to detach her mind. Her hand would move automatically.

Anyone who has stared, hypnotized, into the embers of a glowing fire and been transported out of self to gain insights into other realities has done something similar. The writing, painting, and drawing which result have been regarded as flashes of telepathy. Some claim an origin from some other-worldly source, but as one clairvoyant and trance medium, Eileen Garrett, suggested, the "communications" are from the unconscious mind — in her words, they are "working symbols of the subconscious."

Nicoll was aided in her discoveries by a book, Peter Martin's *Experiment in Depth.* Her results had a Gothic, spooky quality. She found the violent and peculiar inside herself, and eventually recognized these feelings as a source of power. "Nothing is lost," she said. For the first time in her art she felt as though she could breathe. She continued to make automatic drawings daily from 1946 to 1957, regarding them as a way of learning art's scales in anticipation of cohesive works, as piano exercises prepare for music. The automatic drawings helped break down her academic prejudices, and led to a major move in her work into abstraction.

By 1948 Alexandra Luke, helped also by Macdonald, began experimenting with small inkblot-like works. Her images, less sinister than Nicoll's, often have a comic note (she thought of kitchen objects sometimes, such as frying pans). Like Macdonald and Nicoll, however, Luke soon found herself using primordial imagery: the fish, the bird. Central images occurred often in her work as they did in Macdonald's, and perhaps because her medium involved water, as did the others, she constantly used images of water, the great symbol of the unconscious. Luke found automatics a great release, although she, like Macdonald, was already an abstract artist.

Mitchell was first introduced to automatism by her friend Nicoll. All she needed was a hint. That, plus a visit in 1950 to New York where she saw the work of Marc Chagall and Paul Klee, made her open her mind to a new kind of art. Like the others she found automatics meant a form of advanced play that provided the composition with a sense of organic movement and the work with greater freedom. Mitchell, more than the others perhaps, seems to have discovered metaphors of personal identity in the technique. They were a way of touching base with her mind.

Mitchell's results were not as frightening as Nicoll's but more like Luke's — playful and happy. Through automatism she reached back to the girl she once was, putting aside years of hard work and ill health. For her, the final result was an intense realization of the *élan vital,* the life force flowing through all things, or as Dylan Thomas described it, "the force which through the green fuse drives the flower." Her distinctive vocabulary combines an imagery of shallow depth, loosely drawn and painted, with happy hues and passages of bright color. Her floating, almost dancing forms, seem to emerge from a sea or sky. Often in her mature works, line has a life of its own. She particularly enjoys pouring a darker color over a lighter background, then, with a pen, lightly touching up the forms which result — people, birds, dogs, cats, sheep, a fish. These crowded forms in an apparent state of flux provide a glimpse into the artistic process itself.

Mitchell never became a fully abstract artist. For her, as for earlier Canadian painters such as Pegi Nicol MacLeod, people count. A keen sensibility about the figure dominates her work. That she combines it with coordinating flat shapes across the page emphasizes her position as a modernist who kept her visible surroundings firmly in mind. In a way, her watery fields distantly recall the imagery of the American painter William Baziotes, or the use of her surroundings may occasionally suggest Klee or Chagall without ever quoting them directly.

Janet Mitchell is one of several Canadian artists — Ivan Eyre, William Kurelek, and Louis de Niverville are among the others — who carved their own ways of being in a time when purely abstract art seemed not only omnipresent but inevitable. She has made an art of remarkable consistency and true subtlety which joyously celebrates life.

JOAN MURRAY

INTRODUCTION

The story of Janet Mitchell's life and art is a story of persistent, driving determination and single-minded purpose based upon her simple, overwhelming need to paint.

She is largely self-taught, and has struggled alone to find answers to artistic questions that she herself has posed. It has been a long, arduous quest, quietly undertaken in the face of many obstacles and hardships, but it has been and continues to be, the navigational north star of her life. The development of her painting, therefore, has been inextricably interwoven with the development of the person. Now, after more than fifty years of painting, Mitchell continues to grow, to explore new dimensions and new ideas, always straining "to say the truth of things in flowing paint."

The roots of her work are firmly planted along a continuous trail that loops in and around itself in the mountains, prairies, and streets of Western Canada, but it is the unique reality in the mind of Janet Mitchell that provides the inspiration. Like character lines in a face, her paintings are reflections of her life — true extensions of her personality and children of her imagination. Now a master of her craft, she is free to let her ideas fall where they may to create new realities for all who wish to find them.

If one were to produce a book that might be interpreted to be an icon of Mitchell herself, it would be necessary to include more than a retrospective of her artistic development. A more representative and complete approach would interweave work with life, and life with work. Furthermore, it should accomplish this task with honesty, simplicity, unpretentiousness, and humor.

This, then, is the design of *Janet Mitchell: Life and Art.* Biographical narratives and illustrative photographs create an overall framework within which to enjoy Mitchell's poetry, conversation, and painting. The primary source of material for this work was a series of informal conversations that took place during 1989 between Janet Mitchell and me.

From the standpoint of the artistic community, a book about Janet Mitchell is long overdue. The accumulation of detail offered here is intended to remedy this lack by documenting the work of this important Canadian artist. The book also reveals the power, persistence, and strength of a remarkable human spirit.

I paint and paint
and feel depressed
because my hands
cannot express
in paint
the rain that greys the day
and greens the grass
and makes my childish heart
give praise.

To say to say
the truth of things
in flowing paint —
the rain-made rings
in pools,
and steady sounds on roofs,
and swishings underfoot,
and tinkling in the stovepipes
with rhythm.

To paint to paint
the anthem of the rain,
the music in the anthem,
the music in the lane.
To paint
the perfumed air so soft,
and bright reflections
of neon lights on walks
so gay.

JANET MITCHELL

1

MITCHELL'S EARLY YEARS 1912-1933

A little girl stares out from a photograph. She is scrubbed, starched, and stiffly posed in the manner of days gone by. She is almost three years old and she is wearing a new coat and bonnet from Miss Fraser's, the only children's clothing store in town. The store-bought finery and the slight twist of nervousness around her mouth indicate the importance of the picture-taking event, but the occasion, like the photograph, belongs in the past. It was nearly seventy-five years ago.

Janet Mitchell at age 3

The photograph looks somehow unreal in its shades of black and white, but Mitchell's memory, which has no such color limitation, paints the coat "a beautiful shade of blue." She recalls it wistfully, as if it symbolizes a fleeting time of happiness and security for her, when she was the center of her family's universe and the world was a kind and loving place.

The girl in the photograph looks blankly at the woman she has become, her small, round face oblivious to the gaze of the older and wiser eyes examining her. The older Janet Mitchell is a tiny person, small of bone and stature, with sparkling blue eyes and a sweet face, rather like the impossibly cute grandmothers on television commercials. Her hair, which used to be a dark auburn red, is now a soft grey and the bulky brace encasing her right leg from foot to hip reminds me of the way a clumsy, makeshift splint might look on a sparrow. For the time being, her leg must be kept straight because it has no knee.

Mitchell has pulled this picture of herself as a small child from a large cardboard box containing a jumble of photographs that mark a trail through her life, like eskers from a receding glacier. They are nostalgia — friends, hurts, triumphs, sadnesses, and memories. And it is apparent after only a short conversation that they are also, in Mitchell's mind, only history. This remarkable artist, this woman of extraordinary character, has not become what she is today by dwelling on the past.

Fate had been grudgingly kind to the young Janet Mitchell in the photograph. Her birth certificate shows that she was born in Medicine Hat, Alberta, on November 24th, 1912, to a Canadian father and an English mother. The fact that their names were listed separately on the document leads Mitchell to believe they were not married. She never knew them. For a short time the baby girl was cared for by a young doctor and his wife from the Medicine Hat area, but Mitchell does not know who they were or why they were unable to keep her. Her new parents were a childless, Scottish couple from Calgary who took the baby into their home to raise as their own. It is their name she carries.

John and Janet Mitchell had come from Glasgow, Scotland only a few years before. They were an older couple — John was thirty-three and his wife was forty-three when they adopted the little girl. Janet came from a "very proper Scottish family." They were strict Presbyterians who heartily disapproved of a number of things, most of them having to do with entertainment. John was a short, wiry Scotsman who packed his pipe with MacDonald's Briar tobacco, swore mightily at the slightest provocation, and never allowed the facts to interfere with the telling of a good story. He worked for the federal government in the mail room of the Canadian Pacific Railway in the old train station beside the Palliser Hotel.

Janet Mitchell Sr.

The Mitchells were a hard-working, honest couple who lived in a small bungalow in a neighborhood known as Sunnyside. It was a colorful area in the central part of what was then a very small city, a working class district populated mostly by immigrants from Scotland and England. They must have been delighted with the new addition to their family and, for a time, all was well in their small, Sunnyside home.

"When I look back on it now," Mitchell recalls, "I realize I was very precious to those two people. I had scarlet fever when I was six, going on seven, and when I went into the hospital, I had never bathed myself up to that time. She had always helped me. Her sisters were dressmakers of Scottish training, and they used to make some of my clothes for me. It wasn't lavish, because they were poor people. My life would have been so different had she lived."

Mitchell was nine years old when her adoptive mother died. She can't remember her very well, yet she still speaks of her with affection. There were many times in the difficult years that followed that made her long for the love and security that she associated with her "mother."

Her father did what he could to look after her within his modest means and limited experience with children. Sometimes he was able to manage a housekeeper, but often he had no help at all. Although it was a helter-skelter existence, the difficulties seem to have nurtured a special affection between the two of them. Mitchell's memories of her foster father are fuil of walks, parades, bands, wonderful stories, and, as she often comments with great admiration, impressive profanity.

Sergeant John Mitchell,
Calgary Highlands, c 1925
Glenbow Archives

"On Wednesday nights," Mitchell recalls, "my foster father would walk, with me holding his hand, from our little house in Sunnyside to the Calgary Armouries. He was a quartermaster sergeant with the 10th Battalion, Calgary Highlanders and a very proud Scotsman who really knew how to swagger the kilt.

"Rather than leave me alone in the house, he took me with him. I would sit on the balcony above the parade square and watch the maneuvering and listen to band music. When I became tired, I slept on two chairs in the Battalion storeroom and listened to the laughter of the men as they told dirty stories that I did not understand.

"Later, we would walk back home, and if it was the autumn of the year, he stopped at the rented out garden plots on the way. Most of the gardens grew potatoes, but some had cabbages, turnips, and other things. He would help himself to the vegetables and they would end up in his next pot of Scotch broth. He bragged about his soup, saying 'You can dance on it, it is so thick!' On nights when we didn't have Scotch broth, we often had fish and chips, another of his specialties. He was also proud of his tea making. 'It's as black as the ace of spades,' he would say. To this day, I am not fond of Scotch broth or fish and chips.

"He smoked a pipe and chewed MacDonald's plug tobacco. His teeth were black from the tea and tobacco, but he still had all of them when he died at age fifty-six. Out of that mouth of dark teeth came a colorful vocabularly. He was forever going to 'break my bloody neck,' but that was the extent of any punishment I ever had from him — only words.

"He worked night duty and on nights when I wasn't asleep before he left, he would take me with him. I would spend the night in the baggage room sleeping on a shelf with the mailbags, listening to the trains and the conversation of the baggagemen.

"Today, he would no doubt have been declared an unfit person to care for a small girl who was not his own child. I look back with gratitude that I shared his life during those years when I was nine to twelve. He was a good man."

Young Janet must have been something of a handful during the time she was alone with her foster father. John Mitchell worked at night and slept all day, and Janet, like so many bright children, began to explore the fascinating possibilities of the world around her. She was able to do it with a freedom that may have been unusual for children at that time.

Life in Sunnyside was not dull. Most of the residents in the 1920s had emigrated from the British Isles, either just before the First World War or just after. The Scottish people outnumbered the English and Irish, and the Sunnyside kids learned a lot from them.

Three branches of one particular family remain in Mitchell's mind. They were from Edinburgh. At the head of the clan was old Grannie Allan, a widow who was known in the community as a midwife.

"In those days, children were never concerned about mothers with big stomachs," Mitchell remembers. "However, we did take note when Grannie Allan moved in with her suitcase to a particular house. Some way or another, she was responsible for another new baby arriving at that house. We were not sure just how, but rumor had it that she took the baby out of the belly button. It was all very hush-hush.

"After the infant was born, the blinds were drawn so that the mother and babe could rest. Six weeks later, weather permitting, the babe would be put on the veranda in a wicker baby carriage for its nap, and God help the neighborhood kid who made any noise to wake it up."

"Six of Grannie Allan's grandchildren had red hair and were very freckled. Their father had a Ford touring car and on Sundays they would all go fishing in some distant area.

"The rest of us would stand around watching the loading," Mitchell recalls, "and sometimes another kid or two would be invited to go along.

"The children of the families that came out after the war taught us some Scottish jokes and limericks — mostly dirty. I remember there was an Aunty Mary in the clan. We would stand in the garden and sing 'Aunt Mary had a canary/Up the leg of her troosers . . . .' Aunty Mary would come out and threaten us with all sorts of terrible consequences if we didn't stop.

"We also liked to get into the parlor of one of the family homes. The door was usually closed, but on the odd occasion when we managed to get in there, the kids in the family would show us an ornament of two bears that twirled around, and when it was twirled very fast, it would become two bears copulating."

As Mitchell said, she learned a lot from British culture.

There weren't many books on the shelves in John Mitchell's Sunnyside home, but his daughter considered everything there to be fair game. "We had a wonderful doctor's book. Oh, a beautiful doctor's book, with all kinds of pictures in it," Mitchell told me. "I'd get this book out and kind of educate the kids in the neighborhood. I remember my dad catching me once or twice, and he was so mad at me! I have no doubts about kids. I think they're awful, because I remember from my own experience."

News of the World was another source of information. "I don't think my foster mother would have approved of it," said Mitchell. "I'd scare the daylights out of myself. Terrible murders! Oh they were so gruesome! I can see some of the pictures yet. It was the most ghastly paper!"

What was perhaps more significant was the ultimate effect of one particular book. It was a thick book, bound in bright red, about people who had "made it good," that is people who had become successful at various things in spite of incredible hardships.[1] Mitchell was about eleven years old when she read it, and she was influenced by these stories. Certainly the course that Mitchell's life eventually took would have made a story worthy of inclusion in that book.

Those early years gave little indication of Mitchell's future calling as a painter. Her world was confined to the small microcosm of Sunnyside with occasional forays into other parts of the city. The arts had no place in the life of John Mitchell, and exposure to cultural activities was confined to those of a strictly military nature.

Yet, with the advantages of hindsight, it is possible to identify some important elements that may have encouraged the growth of the artistic embryo. Mitchell's loss of her foster mother at an early age forced her to become more independent and self-sufficient than she might have been otherwise. It also enured her to being "different" from the other kids, a perspective that she now believes laid the groundwork for her creative development and integrity. Certainly, with her father either sleeping or working, she would have been freed to a large extent from any highly restrictive traditions of child rearing.

On a more concrete level, it was Mitchell's great fortune to receive what she now remembers as being fairly good art instruction in elementary school. A man by the name of Reg Harvey was hired as a special art instructor by the Calgary School Board to go from school to school to give the students specialized art instruction. Because there weren't many schools at that time, it worked well. Mitchell began painting with watercolors in grade three and she was good at it from the start. The glow of a wonderful moment when a teacher held up one of her paintings in front of the class still warms her face when she speaks of it.

Mitchell was twelve years old when Rose, the housekeeper, moved in. Rose Blenman was something of a tragic figure. Her husband had walked out on her, leaving her with two children and no means of support. She was forced to put them up for adoption and go to work. Rose was acutely resentful that she had been forced to give up her children only to look after someone else's child. To be fair, Mitchell was probably equally resentful about Rose's intrusion into her relationship with her father. However, a situation that would have been difficult under the best of circumstances was made unbearable by Rose's bitterness and harsh treatment of the young teenager.

It wasn't long until John and Rose were living together. They could not marry because of the seven-year-separation period required by law before Rose could be divorced from her first husband. Although they married eventually, the initial arrangement was not easily tolerated by the morally strict community, and the vulnerable adolescence of young Mitchell made her painfully aware of the "shame and disgrace" of it all.

Rose's continual stream of verbal abuse was difficult, but even more bewildering was the fact that John did little to intervene on behalf of his daughter. Mitchell remembers one humiliating occasion in grade eight, when the school board was trying to save money by having the students buy their own books. Rose, however, instructed her foster daughter to inform the school that her father could not afford the purchase. After undergoing grilling by her teachers concerning her father's job and family circumstances, Mitchell was told that she would not be an exception, and her father would have to buy her books. But he didn't. It was a great embarrassment for a child. "I suffered no end of incidents like that — all kinds of them," Mitchell recalls. "She was always rubbing it in that I didn't belong to John Mitchell. I just didn't belong there. Something that I learned early in life is the hold women can have over men. She really had the hold over him, there was no doubt about it. She had a vile temper; she threw scissors at me! I wasn't allowed to go anywhere. It was a horrible life!"

Anyone who knows Janet Mitchell today might speculate that she may not have been the most docile of teenagers under any circumstances, let alone conditions such as those imposed upon her by Rose. At any rate, one day when John and Rose were away, fourteen-year-old Janet packed her bags and moved to the Symons' place down by the Elbow River near the Holy Cross Hospital.

Mrs. Symons, who was crippled with arthritis, was badly in need of help to manage the house and care for her eighteen-month-old baby. Art Symons worked with Mitchell's father in the baggage room. He knew something of the situation between Rose and her stepdaughter and, in spite of John's disapproval, agreed to provide Mitchell with room and board in return for housekeeping and babysitting services.

Mitchell had just finished grade nine at Crescent Heights School and she had been a good student, but there was never any question of whether or not her education would continue. It would not.

"Rose didn't approve of educating girls," Mitchell said. "Her idea was that you get them out to work, and that's it. You see, I was cut off. She figured it was time that I was bringing money into that house."

After about a year, Mitchell left the Symons to work for a Miss Cummings, "a good person" who ran a rooming house just south of Calgary's small Chinatown east of Centre Street. Miss Cummings was also completely crippled with arthritis, and Mitchell was paid ten dollars a month to look after her and clean rooms. Each week, Rose visited her to collect what she had earned, leaving her with stern admonitions and just enough money for a few streetcar tickets. Mitchell didn't go out often. When she could, she liked to visit a friend or go to the young people's group at Knox United Church.

At 16 Janet Mitchell was a housekeeper looking after invalids

The passage of time has not cushioned the feeling of hopelessness and despair she felt in those unhappy years. The deliberate destruction of youthful dreams and hopes cannot be forgiven easily. Mitchell speaks of that period in her life with great difficulty, her eyes bright with remembered hurt. What Rose was relentlessly telling her was that she could have no expectations from life — that her lot was cast and her duty was to obey.

This kind of persecution would be difficult for even those of the most stoic character to ignore. It perhaps explains Mitchell's life-long tendency to expect very little from anybody or anything and to accept anything that does come with great pleasure and surprise. However, she has avoided the kind of bitterness and resentment that might have soured others faced with the same situation. In a way, although it was a hard lesson, the fact that she learned to rely only on herself was an important strength, considering the path that her life would take. She believes the harshness of those teenage years also contributed to the drive and determination that would be necessary factors to her development as an artist. Furthermore, she discovered that her paintings could be a wonderful, temporary escape from the dreariness of her days.

After about a year, Mitchell was able to persuade her father to allow her to spend a year at the commercial business school run by the public school board. She enjoyed her days in the big brick building that housed the school, near the No. 1 Firehall, and found that learning bookkeeping, business English, and shorthand was a great improvement over cleaning rooms.

Many years later when she was well on her way to becoming an important artist, Illingworth Kerr, who was a prominent Western Canadian artist and instructor, commented on the calligraphy detail in her paintings.

"And just when did you study Chinese brush work?" he demanded brusquely, as was his manner.

"I didn't," she replied. "I studied Pittman shorthand."

Mitchell emerged from her year at business school into the dismal economic climate of Calgary during the Depression years. Because there were no jobs available that would allow her to use her new skills, she was forced back into the laborious world of housekeeper. During the next three summers she cleaned cabins in Banff and worked as a chambermaid at Lake Louise. Her winters were spent cleaning houses and looking after arthritic invalids in a series of Calgary homes where she continued to work for room and board, and ten dollars a month.

It was during this time that Rose died of a heart attack. It is not surprising that Mitchell felt no grief. The clouds of disapproval, censure, and dislike that had so stifled her life were suddenly lifted. A difficult chapter was over. Although she could see nothing in her future but an endless round of scrubbing and cleaning, her spirit was strong, and the world became a more exciting, amusing place for the young girl who was not yet twenty years old.

NOTES

1. Mitchell believes this book was called *Pushing Forward.* She remembers clearly that it was offered as an incentive to new subscribers of *The Calgary Herald* sometime in the 1920s. *The Herald* library, unfortunately, does not have a record of it but other sources indicate that it was a time when the newspaper often solicited new subscriptions by offering gifts.

2

EMERGENCE OF THE ARTIST 1933-1949

Garbage cans
back yards
and Alley Cats,
Fences broken
weeds unending.
Neighbors
conscious only
of the street side
neat and tidy.

JANET MITCHELL

In 1933, one year after the death of Rose, John Mitchell married for the third time. Mitchell recalls with amusement, "He was just a little Scotsman, only about five foot six inches. But he had something, didn't he? It wasn't money. Don't forget that women didn't have much of a chance of making it on their own in those days. That was certainly a part of it. Marriage was very attractive, no matter what the guy was like."

Like Mitchell's first foster mother, Elizabeth Maude Mitchell (called Maude or, as Mitchell pronounces it, with her tongue in her cheek, "Mawde") was also ten years older than John. She had been married before and had one grown son living in Edmonton. Mitchell remembers that she was a marvellous person — a pompous English woman who had no use for any religion but the Church of England. "Anybody else was a nonconformist, and she said it with disdain. I was a nonconformist. Yet she was very kind to me. She said she always wished she had a daughter."

With the advent of Maude, circumstances were so much improved that Mitchell moved back home to an area known as Bankview in the southwest part of Calgary. Now she could find work that did not involve room and board.

In 1933, John and Maude celebrated their foster daughter's twenty-first birthday in a big brick house overlooking the city, with verandas upstairs and down. Mitchell's birthday gift was a box of oil paints.

The artistic embryo began to develop. The process was so gradual that Mitchell cannot remember exactly when or how it began. It is likely, however, that the oils in that first box of paints were important catalysts. At some point she began copying postcards. Soon she was carrying a pad and pencil with her when she went out, stopping to sketch here and there as she wound her way through the back alleys to and from work. She knew instinctively that she would not find what she was looking for in the "neat and tidy" front streets of the city. She believed that it was in the unkempt, unguarded, unknown back way where, for her, the "truth of things" lay hidden.

The Mitchells moved out of their Bankview home in 1935 to live in a large house just west of the center of town, near the old McDougall School that is now used for the Alberta provincial government offices. The home belonged to Maude's widowed sister-in-law from her first marriage. Although Mitchell is not certain now of the exact circumstances, she believes that Maude and John agreed to rent a portion of the house so that the sister-in-law would not have to live alone. Their foster daughter moved there with them. One of her few memories about that house is of two photographs hanging on the living room wall. One was a picture of the sister-in-law's first husband (she had been married twice); immediately beside it, in stubborn photographic equality, was a picture of her late husband's first wife.

In 1936, Mitchell was hired as a chambermaid by the Palliser Hotel. It was hard work, and she remembers very clearly that her daily tasks included making up seventeen beds. In fact, she developed such a distaste for the chore that she has never again made her own bed on a daily basis.

Her official explanation is that it is a waste of time that could be better spent doing other things, but if pressed she admits that the real reason is simply that she detests doing it because of her days as a hotel chambermaid.

Although the work at the Palliser was hard, Mitchell's life changed. Like a small bird being given its freedom from a cage, Mitchell began to stretch her wings to explore farther and farther afield, leaving behind the psychological limitations that had been imposed upon her by Rose. On her noon lunch break at the hotel she could be found with her nose buried in a book of French grammar. Every morning she left for work early so that she could sketch in the streets, roads, and alleys on the way. Every evening she arrived home late with her pad full of drawings and her mind humming with ideas. Soon she began to realize how much she didn't know and started taking art lessons, at fifty cents a lesson, from a Ruby Brown, whose calling as an artist, in Maude's eyes, was redeemed only by the fact that she was the daughter of a Calgary minister.

Mitchell sketched on her way home from work as a chambermaid, c 1936

Mitchell did not choose Brown to be her teacher because of her formal art training at the Institute of Technology and Art. She was not even aware that Brown had been a student of A.C. Leighton. These kinds of considerations were beyond her artistic understanding at that time. Quite simply, she wanted to take art lessons and Ruby Brown was someone she knew who gave them. The fact that Brown was well qualified to introduce Mitchell to some of the basics of art was simply a lucky accident.

"Ruby Brown was a traditionalist," Mitchell says. "She had me sketching outdoors, doing old barns and learning a bit about perspective. That was the beginning. She was doing things the way they should be done, and I learned something about that from her. I think it was a good place for me to start."

Mitchell's lessons ended within a few years when Brown moved to Vancouver, but Mitchell visited her there several times to go on weekend sketching trips. In the meantime, her life began to fall into two distinct categories of time: when she could sketch and when she couldn't.

John Mitchell died of cancer in 1939 at the age of fifty-six. After fifteen months of caring for him at home during his illness, Maude and Mitchell were grief-stricken and exhausted. Their loss, however, soon became secondary to the hard question of how to survive without John's salary. He had worked for the government for almost twenty years, but there was no pension for his widow, only a single superannuation payment of three thousand dollars. At the age of sixty-six, Maude had no other source of income. Her son from her first marriage had ignored her for years and continued to do so for the rest of her life. The enormous burden of supporting them both was placed squarely upon Mitchell's shoulders and it remained there for the next twenty-eight years.

The wages of a hotel chambermaid were no longer adequate and Mitchell left her job at the Palliser to take comptometer training at Henderson's Business College. The comptometer was a wonderful new business machine that could add, divide, multiply, and subtract — a forerunner of the more sophisticated calculating machines that followed it. Because of her knowledge of the use of this device as well as her previous business school training, Mitchell was hired as a clerk with the Calgary Office of the Income Tax Department in 1940, her place of employment for the next twenty-two years. Her days of making beds were finally over.

First art teacher, Ruby Brown (left) and Mitchell, 1939

Her salary at the Income Tax Department was not large and the rent that they had been paying to Maude's sister-in-law was quite beyond Mitchell's means. She and Maude were forced to move into the tiny shack-like house with the dirt basement back in Sunnyside. The first Mrs. Mitchell had bought it during the First World War and had lived there with John when he came back from his service overseas in 1918. John had also lived there with Rose. Maude, however, had refused to move into the house, and so it had been rented out.

The years of time and tenants had taken their toll on what had always been a very modest structure. Maude was not at all pleased with the circumstances in which she found herself, but Mitchell was stoically realistic. They simply had no alternative.

There was a decrepit little barn at the back of the house that Mitchell could use as an uncomfortable but functional studio space. She bought a small radiant heater for warmth and, one windy spring morning, went out to turn it on for a while before beginning a day of painting. On her way back to the house, she stopped and stared in amazement. One side of the dirt basement had caved in during the night. Her first reaction was to laugh uproariously. There was something about the fact that a substantial portion of the foundation of their home and hearth could totally disintegrate without even waking them up that struck her as being remarkably funny. She had no idea how she was going to pay for repairs; the small house was already in dismal condition. Maude was not amused.

Mitchell, even then, had an extraordinary ability to stand far enough back from adversity to be able to look for the fun and humor in things, an ability that has remained an important part of her life and art over the years. "I think the drama and contrasts of a person's life (and I have certainly had the contrasts) are important," Mitchell relates, "but I think the humor has always been there for me, and I think that's what has shown up in my painting. Maybe that's what has carried me through. I was watching. I was seeing the funny things as I went along in my life."

In more psychological terms, this ability might be associated with a well-balanced personality capable of maintaining a rational perspective in difficult situations. Mitchell has dealt with many hardships but she has never been overcome by them. Perhaps humor has been one of her most important defenses, and because it is such an integral part of her personality, it is inevitably also an integral part of her art.

For the next ten years the fabric of Mitchell's life was woven with two distinct threads: her role as a breadwinner was the warp of the fabric; the weft was her continual struggle to learn her art. She derived great satisfaction from both.

"I was always conscientious about my job," Mitchell insists. "I went in there as a steno, but I didn't do any steno work. I was put in the filing room for two years. I got moved on to assessing sometime in the war years. Nowadays they call them auditors. At first, they were certain that women couldn't do that sort of thing, but during the war they were short of men. There were three women who got charged with assessing the simple returns. I remember the Director, Sandy Alexander, passing by the door and saying, 'Be sure to read the Act like it was your Bible' (he pronounced it the Scottish way — 'Byble'). Later, I was in charge of the group. I did the toughest ones."

At noon hours, at night, on weekends, and during holidays, Mitchell sketched and painted. She began to gravitate towards the small centers of artistic activity in the city. Her first encounter was through the Calgary Sketch Club, which she joined in 1936. The Club rented a studio for ten dollars a month on the second floor of a building on 8th Avenue in the heart of downtown Calgary.

"I remember that Picardy's was on the street level," Mitchell said. "It was a well-known eating place for light lunches and teas. Jimmie Bird had his advertising display workshop on the first flight up. One of his business projects was to do the advertising billboards for the movies at the Capitol Theatre twice a week. Jimmie was a member of the Sketch Club.

"Across the hall, Ernie King had his tailoring establishment. Calgarians always knew when spring had arrived when they saw him walking down 8th Avenue in his cream flannel suit and straw bowler hat.

"Up another flight of stairs was the Sketch Club studio. It had a large window facing north, overlooking 8th Avenue. From it we could look into the windows of the St. Regis Hotel and down the avenue to the bright lights of the Capitol Theatre. Directly below, we could see ordinary citizens, military men and women, pre-war Chevrolets and Fords, and, of course, the streetcars.

"Sketch Club members were a youngish lot, full of creative enthusiasm and ambition. Many became distinguished in their fields of the visual arts. In those war years, one or two armed servicemen would come and participate in the activities until being posted elsewhere. There was also a Mr. Boot — an Englishman — who was quite a character. Old Mr. Boot would go out on sketching trips and he'd have a great big umbrella, a fancy stool, and a fancy easel. He really rigged himself up. The Club was special. Conversation and exchange of ideas were the stimulant for all of us. Sometimes we would gather at a large, round table at the nearby White Lunch and sit there all night talking over a cup of coffee.

"At one of the parties in the studio, the members had been requested to bring a cartoon to decorate the walls. Matt Lindstrom, who was known for his wild animal mountain paintings, brought cartoons about most of the members. They were very funny and clever, which surprised us all because Matt was a dour man who had immigrated from Finland in the Depression years. He told the story about how he practised his meager knowledge of English on the boat coming to Canada. His arrival at the destination to which immigration authorities had assigned him was very distressing for him because he understood not a word that anyone said. He thought he had been sent to the wrong country until someone told him he was in a French-speaking community at St. Paul, Alberta.

"The time came, however, when the rent for the Sketch Club studio doubled to twenty dollars a month. That was too much to pay, so we moved out. Later we met at the old Coste House in Mount Royal."

The Sketch Club was good for Mitchell. For the first time in her life, she found herself among people who shared her interest in art, who knew something about it, and who encouraged her. It was a heady experience for a young woman who for so many years had worked completely alone. There had never been any question in her mind that she would not continue, but the close social ties and support she found through the Sketch Club were very welcome.

In addition, for the first time since Ruby Brown, she received some instruction, this time from none other than the well-known Alberta landscape artist, Henry Glyde.

Glyde was an art teacher with the Provincial Institute of Technology and Art, which later became the Southern Alberta Institute of Technology. Because the Department's building on Calgary's north hill was being used for armed services training, the program and its instructors had been temporarily relocated in the Coste House, a magnificent old home on the slopes of the prestigious neighborhood of Mount Royal.

Although Mitchell took only a life drawing class from Glyde, she believes she was strongly influenced by him in her early painting. "He was a very formal artist," she recalls, "but that didn't matter to me then because I didn't know anything. It wasn't a matter of choice anyway; it was just that his class was available to me. Looking back now, I'm sure that his formal approach was a good thing for me at that time. I needed to know those things.

"Some of my early watercolor paintings were strongly influenced by Glyde. For example, he always had his poles going crooked in his paintings, and the watercolor with which I won the scholarship to the Banff summer school — *Back Entrance of a Chinese Laundry* (1942) — had crooked poles as well. He was very stylized."

When the Art Department moved back to its home on the hill after the war, the Coste House became Calgary's first public fine arts center. Mitchell decided to rent a space there, which she did for the significant sum of five dollars a month. At night after work and on weekends she walked from her Sunnyside house to the big house in Mount Royal to paint. Her little studio placed her in the very center of the arts in Calgary. For Mitchell the Coste House was a special place. There was always so much going on — handicraft groups with looms upstairs; on the main floor recitals or lectures; in the lower area a play rehearsal; and model railway men in the attic.

"It was a great time," says Mitchell, "because there was an intermingling of the different arts. When there was a poetry reading, we'd all go to poetry reading. We went to symphonies and we went to the Canadian Drama Festival, which was held at the Grand Theatre. You'd go into the tea room at the Coste House afterwards, and there'd be this conglomeration of people in different fields of the arts. It was great!

"In a way, it's much better today because there are so many more things going on. You have a choice now. Yet, maybe it was better then because there was no choice. You took in everything that was going on. Now you couldn't begin to do that, so maybe you sometimes don't see as much."

Working at the Coste House provided Mitchell with the opportunity to continue her work and to associate with other artists in the community. But because it was a microcosm of the other arts as well, it also exposed her to things such as music, poetry, dance, drama, and literature. It gave her an awareness of the arts that she had not had before and which she has continued to expand and enjoy throughout her lifetime.

Mitchell's entry into Calgary's artistic community introduced her to exciting new ideas not previously available to her. However, it was the art of the Group of Seven and of Emily Carr that she now identifies as being the first significant milestone in her artistic awareness. She remembers first seeing paintings by these artists in an exhibition in the Stampede grandstand, held in conjunction with the Calgary Stampede. "I had never seen anything like it in my life," she remembers. "I think it changed everything for me. I couldn't believe that I was seeing this in the Stampede grandstand. When I look back on it now, I am amazed that they allowed a show like that in there, so unprotected. But it showed me a new world that I knew nothing about."

The work on those canvases was a revelation to Mitchell. She had never before considered the possibility that there could be new, artistically legitimate ways of looking at things. The revolutionary interpretations of Canadian landscapes hanging in the Stampede grandstand presented her with ideas that she had not yet encountered in the narrow world of traditional art to which she had been confined. It was an exciting discovery.

Some of Mitchell's early paintings reflect the influence of the work she saw at that show. Once she had been exposed to the innovative ideas on those canvases, they became part of her learning experience. She explored them with enormous enthusiasm.

Mitchell was now in her late twenties. She was supporting her widowed stepmother, but she had what was considered to be a good job (the phrase "for a woman" was always attached). She had a place to live, a place to paint, and a keen awareness of how much more she wanted to know.

The decade of the forties was a time of apprenticeship and learning for Mitchell. It was also a time of new friendships and associations with other artists who would provide her with support and encouragement for many years to come.

She enrolled in night classes at the Provincial Institute of Technology and Art, where she studied life drawing with Illingworth ("Buck") Kerr. Kerr, who was the head of the Art School at the Institute, was widely respected for both his paintings and his instruction. Although he was never known for his diplomacy in or out of the classroom, he and Mitchell developed a grudging friendship that lasted until he died in 1989. She has many stories about it. She says that even after she was an established artist, Kerr always ridiculed the "primitive" way she drew the figures in her paintings. On one particular occasion she answered spiritedly, "Well, I took life drawing from you up at the college, didn't I?"

He didn't say much then but later in the evening he told her that he wished there were other students who had learned the way she did. This, she believes, was the first positive comment he had ever made to her about her work. She was enormously pleased. Much later, Kerr attended a party celebrating Mitchell's honorary doctoral degree. Mitchell was called upon to make a speech. With a twinkle in her blue eyes, she announced to the gathering of prominent Calgary artists and art appreciators, "I'd like to thank Buck Kerr, who has taught me everything I know about drawing figures."

Luke Lindoe in Salmon Arm, 1946

Mitchell respected Kerr, but she doesn't think he had any influence on her work. "I wasn't out doing landscape painting with him." she said. "I was, again, doing figure drawing. And again, it was the same thing — learning the basics about perspective, form, shape, and all the other things. Certainly with Glyde there was an influence. And with Ruby Brown, because she was my first teacher. But Kerr — I can't think there was any influence at all."

The Lindoes, however, provided a long friendship that had an important influence in Mitchell's artistic development. She had met Luke Lindoe when he was the instructor at a ceramics and sculpture class she took at the Institute of Technology and Art in the early forties.

"I registered in ceramics because I wanted to do anything that might help me understand. It's surprising that I still have that mask [it's propped up against the fireplace hearth in her home after being rescued from her back yard] because Luke usually smashed students' work as soon as he'd given his criticism. 'That's all right,' he'd say, 'you learned something,' and bang! This one, he felt, was creative and good, and so he let me keep it. I really didn't care for the darned thing but somehow it has managed to stick around all these years."

One Sunday afternoon, Lindoe and his wife Vivian invited Mitchell to tea at the Lindoe home. "You know, I've been lucky in that people must have seen something," Mitchell muses. "I don't know what. I don't know how. Because I don't think I had much going for me. I wasn't beautiful. I was kind of shy. Anyway, Luke must have seen some spark, and that was the beginning of a very good friendship."

One of Mitchell's early major painting trips was with the Lindoes, their son, and their dog. It was a chilly British Columbia expedition in a small open boat in the fall of 1945, traveling at six miles an hour through the Shuswap to the head of the Thompson River and camping along the way. "They were a great influence," Mitchell continues. "I learned a different sort of courage — the kind you need in the country. I had just been a city kid all my life and I learned about a different kind of hardship."

"It was silent and beautiful," Mitchell remembers, "We didn't have money for camping equipment, so we lived quite primitively. This was a great learning holiday. It was tough and cold and uncomfortable, but we painted, and we painted. I knew a lot more when I returned to Calgary."

In Mitchell's judgment, Luke Lindoe, a graduate from the Ontario College of Art, was very "Group of Sevenish." She believes that she learned much about landscape painting from him, and some of her paintings from that time seem to reflect his influence. However, when she speaks of the Lindoes, she remembers the more intangible ways they enriched her life.

"The Lindoes were hard workers. Luke always said he was never happier than when he was working. He believed in work. I always have too. I think Luke and Vivian helped me to expand my visual awareness in a very important way. I was such a city girl, and there were so many things that I would never have seen if they hadn't said look at this, 'look at this turtle, see the patterns.' We'd go out swimming at night off the little island at Loon Lake, and we would listen to all the sounds in the island. They helped me learn how to tune in. I think this was very important for me." Through the Lindoes Mitchell met two more people who were to become extremely important to her life and her work — Jim and Marion Nicoll.

The Nicolls were a dashing couple with a large amount of artistic talent and a flair for the exotic. Their work has long been recognized as important. They and the Lindoes had become friends while studying together at art school under A.C. Leighton, another important Western Canadian artist. Marion Nicoll had been Vivian Lindoe's bridesmaid when she was married and, on the honeymoon, the four of them had taken a painting trip together up Ghost River.

After the Nicolls were married, they spent some time out of the province while Jim Nicoll was working as a civilian with the air force. They arrived back in Calgary around 1942. Their little house in Bowness, which was then a small village on the northwest edge of Calgary, was soon the unofficial social headquarters for Calgary's artistic community.

To Mitchell, Marion Nicoll seemed to embody everything that she wanted to be — exciting, traveled, talented, educated, popular, and a good artist. Mitchell had admired her for some time. "I remember going to an exhibition in the Hudson's Bay," she said. "They had what they called a French Room for select things on the second floor. It was where they had art exhibitions. I remember Marion sitting at the desk. I guess she would have been answering questions. I remember seeing her, but I would never have spoken to her. I was too shy."

Jim Nicoll and Toby, c 1946

Luke Lindoe told Marion Nicoll that she should meet Janet Mitchell, so she was invited to dinner. "I had a wonderful evening. Just absolutely wonderful!" Mitchell recalls. "I sat there listening to the two of them for hours, and Marion finally said, 'Janet, the last streetcar runs at twenty-five minutes after eleven.' I was so embarrassed. I suffered for that for a long time — to think that she had to tell me to go home. But she really wasn't, you know. She was just concerned about me getting that last streetcar."

That was the beginning of the Nicoll friendship. Mitchell found the group stimulating. They were teaching at the college in the old army huts and Mitchell rode her bike there sometimes at noon hour from the tax department to have lunch with them.

The Lindoes and Nicolls were like family to Mitchell. They seem to have extended great love and affection to her. As well they were encouraging to her as a fellow artist. Marion Nicoll thought Mitchell's honesty was reflected in her work. She said that when Mitchell painted children, one always stood aside from the crowd, and she believed the lone child was Mitchell. She said that some of Mitchell's paintings terrified her; others were delightful. All in all she believed Mitchell's work was becoming more serious.[1]

In spite of the close friendship Mitchell cannot identify any particular direct influence that the Nicolls had on her painting. But the influence in her life was enormous. "I admired and looked up to the Nicolls in every way — as artists and as people," she said. "Being associated with them socially — their conversation — wonderful conversation — was a great source of stimulation for me." Her greatest gift from the Nicolls, however, was their encouragement. Marion offered outright praise. Jim was more hesitant, but once in a while he would say something positive and when he did, Mitchell felt good about it. She valued the Nicolls' friendship.

Marion Nicoll and Watchy, J.W. (Jock) Macdonald's dog

Mitchell often visited the Nicoll home on the outskirts of the city. "It was seven miles to Bowness — probably five miles to the Nicoll house. The streetcar swayed its way along the flats close along the river to Bowness on the hour. On wintry nights after a session or a dinner at the Coste House, we would drive out there for coffee or hot mulled wine. It was all darkness after leaving the upper Hillhurst street lights, but there was always the anticipated pleasure of good conversation.

"The Nicoll land was quite bare of trees then, in the forties. In the summer, two neighborhood goats kept the grass clipped and ate all the cigarette butts.

"The house was one large room, with a lean-to kitchen and an outside toilet. That was the way they preferred it. When the village of Bowness put in water pipes and sewers in the fifties, Jim offered many wondrous and devastating comments. He disapproved of the modern conveniences encroaching on their land. Before this intrusion of civilization, they obtained their water from a well in the kitchen. You had to lift the lid and put the bucket down. We always feared for Jim (who tended to like his drink) — that sometime he might fall in.

"In summer, there was always a garden party or two for out-of-town visitors or students from the Art College. In winter, there were wonderful parties, especially between Christmas and New Year's. It was a small colony of artists then and we all knew one another. The place was a focal point where many things were thrashed out in sometimes heated arguments. Jim, always so articulate, used the English language like no one else I knew. I used to believe that he spent part of every day with dictionary in hand preparing to throw out some new words to overwhelm the guests.

"I recall so many kind gestures. Once, at a particularly low time in my life, I left by train for the coast. As the train passed by the Nicoll's back garden, there they were out waving to me with colored, batiked flags. Marion sat in her established chair in the corner. Luke Lindoe once said she sat there great and mighty on her throne and we feel obliged to pay homage to her.

"On a Sunday morning between Christmas and New Year's, there was always a breakfast party — spiced beef, great giant olives, and strange foods which were all foreign to me. Marion, having traveled in Europe and studied in London in the thirties, and Jim having been abroad, just had that little extra international flavor that some of us had not yet experienced. They had a sophistication and flair for the unusual. Our minds and appetites were stimulated."

Mitchell's progress as an artist continued. In 1943, she won a scholarship to attend the Banff Summer School, where she was instructed by George Pepper, a Toronto artist with a firm grip on the fundamentals. For the first time in her thirty-one years, she had the opportunity to concentrate all her energies on her work for an extended period of time.

Her fellow students were enthralled by the magnificent Rocky Mountain scenery surrounding them, taking great pains to choose just the right location in which to set up their easels each day. The instructor pedaled a bicycle from student to student, offering his comments and criticisms as he went along. However, it did not take long for Pepper to realize that student Janet would not be found painting the mountains. He would be more likely to find her in the alley concentrating on the back door of Harmon's drug store or one of the other main street stores, working on something she could "get her teeth into."

It was during the forties that Mitchell sold her first work. When a Calgary photographer expressed interest in buying one of her paintings, Mitchell suggested that he might pay her by doing a photograph of her with Maude. A deal was struck. The price of the painting in question was five dollars.

In 1949, Mitchell's earnings as a tax assessor made it possible for her to assume the sixty-five dollars-a-month mortgage of a large home in northwest Calgary. This house had a basement that could be developed into a modest studio so that she could work at home, a feature of no small importance considering the demands on her time, the long cold walk to the Coste House, and her increasingly frail health.

It was also in 1949 that she had her first show at the Breithaupt Gallery in Toronto.

Mitchell's first sale: a painting in exchange for a photograph of herself and Maude

MITCHELL'S ART IN THE FORTIES

Mitchell's art in the forties is probably best described in her own words. "In the beginning, there were years and years of going out sketching, trying to understand, trying to put subject matter as I saw it down on paper or canvas."

The paintings selected here represent an interesting combination of biographical association and artistic experimentation.

Back Entrance of a Chinese Laundry (1942) was a sight Mitchell saw every day on her way to work at the income tax office. It was a little laundry in the alley where the land dipped down just west of Knox United Church. This was the painting that won her a scholarship to attend the Banff School of Fine Arts during the summer of 1943. Looking back at it now, she points out the crooked pole of the clothes line, which she recognizes as resulting from the influence of Henry Glyde, from whom she had taken a night class in life drawing.

Parkhill — Sunday A.M. (1944) is of a similar style. Its location was west of the Burnsland Cemetery on a hill that continued to be a favorite sketching spot for many years.

The location of *Bowness Streetcar Tracks* (1947) was near the home of Mitchell's good friends, Jim and Marion Nicoll. The painting illustrates the more intense color that she was beginning to use in her work.

Some of Mitchell's earliest successful paintings were landscapes painted in oil in 1946 and 1947.[2] *On the Banks of the Thompson River* (1947) is one example. The sketch for this work was done in 1946 while Mitchell was camping on the Indian reservation outside the town of Chase, British Columbia, and the large pallette knife painting was completed a year later. The influence of the Group of Seven and of Luke Lindoe can be seen in this work, which remained in Mitchell's possession until quite recently.

"It is a very vivid painting" Mitchell says. "The yellow is a very bright yellow. Very vigorous. I remember saying to Luke one time years later that I felt maybe I had lost some of the vitality of these early paintings. He told me that without that vitality, I couldn't be doing what I was doing now."

The treatment of the figures, the funnel-like shapes of the tepees, and even the composition in *Indian Village* (1948) are distinct reminders of the work of Emily Carr, another formative influence in Mitchell's painting. "I knew of Emily Carr by then," Mitchell told me, "because of the Stampede show, and I was very influenced by it in many ways. I think she could have done a better job on the figures though. And the tepees. I remember a friend of mine at the Coste House looked at the painting and told me it was perfectly obvious that I didn't know how many poles there were in a tepee because I had far too many. He was right. I didn't. I still don't. How many are there, anyway?"[3]

Early Calgary (1948), painted in the same year as *Indian Village* (1948), is perhaps a hint of the direction that Mitchell would eventually take in her work. It still portrays a recognizable location, which Mitchell identifies as being near the brick house in Bankview where she celebrated her twenty-first birthday, but it is executed with much greater freedom and a more unique style than the other paintings.

Ironically, this painting was described by several critics at the time as reflecting the influence of Ontario artist David Milne, a comparison that has subsequently been made with regard to later Mitchell work as well.[4] The fact is, however, that when Mitchell painted *Early Calgary* (1948), she did not know Milne and had never seen his work. One must therefore conclude that this 1948 painting represents a significant step in the development of her own art.

NOTES

1. Marion Nicoll, "A tribute to Janet Mitchell," *Emerging Arts West,* January, 1976, p. 38.

2. Andrew J. Oko in the Introduction to the catalogue of a retrospective show of Janet Mitchell's work at the Glenbow-Alberta Institute, Calgary, March 2-April 3, 1977.

3. Diamond Jeness, *Indians of Canada,* Toronto, Ontario: University of Toronto Press, 1977, p. 90. This source describes a tepee as being constructed with fourteen to eighteen longpoles, indicating a much larger size than is shown in *Indian Village.* Perhaps, for the size of the Mitchell tepees, the number of poles is just right.

4. See for example, Astrid Twardowski, "Janet Mitchell at the Calgary Allied Arts Centre," *Canadian Art,* XX (4), p. 205.

Back Entrance of a Chinese Laundry (1942)
watercolor, 31.7 x 40.6 cm (12.5 x 16 in)
Mr. and Mrs. Neil A. Ross collection
Photograph by John Dean

Parkhill — Sunday A.M. (1944)
watercolor, 33 x 38 cm (13 x 15 in)
Bennett Jones Verchere collection
Photograph by John Dean

Bowness Streetcar Tracks (1947)
watercolor, 24 x 33 cm (9.5 x 13 in)
Private collection
Photograph by John Dean

On the Banks of the Thompson River (1947)
oil, 65.2 x 75 cm (25.5 x 29.5 in)
Alberta Art Foundation collection
Photograph courtesy of Alberta Art Foundation

Indian Village (1948)
oil, 61 x 76 cm (24 x 30 in)
Private collection

Early Calgary (1948)
watercolor, 30.5 x 31.7 cm (12 x 15.5 in)
Bow Valley Industries Ltd. collection
Photograph by John Dean

3

THE EARLY FIFTIES 1950-1956

Should an artist paint to please
A bunch of football fans or hockeyists
Or cowboy-loving musicers
And consequently have money in his fists
For painting?

Or should an artist paint to please
The intellect of this and yon
Or snobbish up-tee-do's
And so have canvas smeared with goings on
To squizzle?

Paint for the public paint for money.
Paint for the public painting's crummy.
Paint for the artist ain't so funny.
No money's still crummy.

JANET MITCHELL

The questions that Mitchell posed in the above poem are questions that have been asked by struggling artists for centuries. Her answers, which the poem makes very clear, are a crisp summary of her down-to-earth assessment of the situation. She worked at a daily job and she painted.

For the decade following 1950, her existence continued to be this delicate balancing act between two separate, and seemingly contradictory, lives. From 8:15 a.m. to 4:45 p.m. each business day, she was a tax assessor diligently working at her desk; after hours, she was an obsessed artist prowling through the streets and countryside or painting in her basement studio. She wasn't ready yet to gamble on her ability to support herself and her aging foster mother through painting. These years of working and painting marked a time of intense personal struggle, of independent learning and discovery, and of enormous artistic growth.

"When I think of it," Mitchell says, "I don't really think that working in the Income Tax Department and being a painter was that much of a contradiction. Generally, I found it to be quite a stimulating job. I was always good in arithmetic at school. I remember distinctly when I was in grade two, they put a column on the blackboard . . . and I had to add it up in front of the class. I was so quick at it that they brought the principal in to see me do it. I couldn't do it in my head — but if I saw the figures I could do it immediately. A grade eight teacher once told me that I have a million-dollar pencil and a five-cent head."

Mitchell paused and reflected and then continued to speak of her days at the income tax office. "I had to have work. That's just the way it was. But it was a long chunk out of my life when it would have been nice to have had more energy for painting."

There were several milestones in this busy life and one of them was a trip to New York. One of Mitchell's friends in the tax department, who had left in 1948 to study journalism in New York, married and settled down in a home not far from Columbia University where she was continuing her studies. When she invited Mitchell to visit her, Mitchell seized at the opportunity. She applied for an extension of her holidays from three weeks to four, packed her bag, and emptied her savings account to buy a train ticket for her first journey to the world outside Western Canada.

The New York of 1950 was a dazzling, dizzying experience for someone approaching it with the intention of swallowing up everything it had to offer.[1]

From her vantage point forty years later, Mitchell is able to appreciate the degree to which her trip expanded her vision at a time that was ripe for her own development. Not only did it expose her to the riot of ideas and approaches tumbling through the dynamic New York setting, but it also gave her some artistic perspectives that she did not have before, perspectives that have become integral to her work over the years. She saw the work of many artists, but there were three in particular whose painting so strongly influenced her that they earned permanent places of honor in her own artistic vision. The three artists were Vincent van Gogh, Marc Chagall, and Paul Klee.

Mitchell had, of course, seen reproductions of van Gogh paintings before her trip to New York, but the printing process of 1950 was not able to accurately reproduce the dazzling color of his work. Seeing original van Gogh works at an exhibition in the Metropolitan Museum literally took her breath away; her catalogue of the show, which she still keeps on her shelf, is dotted with her astonished notes about the differences in color between the prints and the originals. "I think I gained something spiritually from seeing those paintings at that time," she recalls. "They were just so vibrant and brilliant — like walking into rooms of bright sunlight. I think of van Gogh even when I'm painting today — for example, when I use a very dark sky and light-colored hill — yellows against an almost navy blue sky."

The van Gogh influence allowed an expanded awareness and appreciation of color to burst into Mitchell's artistic consciousness that led to innovative exploration and experimentation. Her work in all media — watercolors, acrylics, and oils — is known for its dynamic, imaginative use of color.

Mitchell was also enthusiastic when she discovered the work of the Swiss artist Paul Klee and the French-Russian painter Marc Chagall. The impact upon her was profound.

Mitchell had been excited by the Group of Seven's personal visions of traditional subjects, that is, their individualistic ways of looking at Canadian landscape. Klee and Chagall took it one step farther by painting personal, almost mystical, visions of non-realistic worlds — worlds of dreams, emotions, and feelings. Seeing their work, Mitchell realized that she did not have to work within the traditional confines of subject matter that had been so firmly established in her own small world of awareness; she could do anything that she wanted to do.

Furthermore, there was a point of communication between the works of these two artists and Mitchell that she had not experienced before. It was because their paintings revealed the artists' inner emotions, a quality that was much more meaningful to her than "cold, academic paintings that had no soul." Seeing the work of Klee and Chagall gave her more definition, more confidence in her own artistic philosophy. It also helped to crystallize the artistic approach that would become so fundamental to her future work.

In retrospect, one might observe that it helped her to discover that the "truth of things" for which she had been searching was to be found only within herself. She expressed it in this way. "Chagall and Klee helped me realize I could just do what was in my inner soul, and that appealed to me so much. Theirs were very personal paintings, and they spoke to me like others didn't. They show a mystical vision of a strange, dream world. To me, seeing that work was a release."

Mitchell speaks about the importance of finding freedom when she is painting, freedom from inhibitions, restrictions, and limitations that allows the participation of the unconscious in the creative process. Before her New York trip she had just begun to explore this idea. By about 1946, her friend and mentor, Marion Nicoll, was experimenting with automatic drawing, a technique in which the artist draws or paints without conscious involvement. Nicoll described it as a way to keep a "path" open to the unconscious.[2] But it was not until Mitchell was exposed to the work of Klee and Chagall that she recognized the importance of the idea with regard to her own work and began to actively investigate ways to accomplish this for herself. Automatic writing, rather than automatic drawing, and techniques of self-hypnosis helped her to find the freedom she wanted in the years to come.

When Mitchell returned from her trip to New York, she went back to her painting with a renewed sense of energy and purpose. Her efforts, however, were temporarily confounded by a serious attack of rheumatic fever that put her in the hospital for three weeks and, when it recurred, for another three weeks. Although the illness was serious in itself, it was the side effect of the prescribed cortizone treatment that evidently had the most significant consequences. Persistent ill health plagued her, probably because of the tuberculosis bacilli that had been activated in her system by the cortizone, but of which she was unaware at the time. In the late summer of 1953, she took a three-month leave of absence from work. Her friends, the Lindoes, offered to let her use their small cabin in British Columbia, and so Mitchell packed her sketchbooks and paints for a solitary three-month sojourn on the shores of Loon Lake, now known as Gardner Lake. Surrounded by the extraordinary beauty and solitude of the area, she filled her days with writing, painting, sketching, and thought.[3]

Mitchell and Skipper on the shore of Loon Lake

Unfortunately, the time came when Mitchell had to leave her haven at Loon Lake to go back to work. Her enthusiasm for her painting, however, had been well nourished by her experiences there. It had been the longest, most intense, period that she had ever devoted to her art without other distractions and obligations, and she was very much encouraged by the growth that she could see in her work.

Her reputation, too, was growing. In 1952, she had been represented in a Canadian exhibition shown in Ottawa for the visit of the Queen Mother. At about that time one of her works, *Celestial Night,* was purchased by the National Gallery of Canada, who used it in its calendar and on a Christmas card. By the spring of 1954 another Mitchell painting, *Moon Over Mountain Village,* had been accepted for the Biennial Show at the National Gallery of Canada and was subsequently purchased by the Gallery. Through this prestigious exposure, a small core of collectors across the country was beginning to become aware of Western Canada's Janet Mitchell, and they liked what they saw.

Just as her career as an artist seemed to be gaining momentum, Mitchell succumbed to tuberculosis. Her coughing, which had been getting worse for months, was aggravated dangerously when she began to work in enamel paints, a medium that she was thoroughly enjoying because of the vividness of the colors. The fumes were devastating to her. After an evening of painting she would be up all night coughing, steaming herself with a kettle, only to have to drag herself to work at the tax department the next day. In February, 1956, she was diagnosed as having tuberculosis and she was sent to the Baker Memorial Sanatorium on the banks of the Bow River for nearly a year.

The enforced rest was a mixed blessing. At first the doctors would not allow her to paint at all, and she found the inactivity to be extremely difficult. "At the end of two months, I couldn't stand it any longer," she remembers. "I got a friend to bring my watercolor box and brushes in. I kept them at the bedside in the drawer, and one night after supper I thought to hell with them, and I got the paints out and did a watercolor. So the next day, I admitted it to the doctors. They gave me permission to work one hour in the morning and one hour in the afternoon."

As her health improved during the next eight months, Mitchell was allowed to spend more time painting. Working in a small room next to her own which she was given to use as a studio, she produced more than one hundred oils and watercolors between April and December.

The news that she was painting again hit the Calgary papers. In an interview with Linda Curtis of *The Calgary Herald,* she commented: "This is an ideal life for an artist. No dishes to wash. No meals to get. No office to go to every day. Nothing to do but rest and paint."[4]

By the time she left the sanatorium, Mitchell had a one-woman show at Robertson Galleries Ltd. in Ottawa as well as one at the Allied Arts Centre in Calgary, twenty watercolors on loan to the Toronto Picture Loan Society, a request for paintings by the Edmonton Picture Loan Society, and invitations to send work for Christmas sales in Toronto, Winnipeg, and Vancouver. At the age of forty-four, she was being "discovered."

MITCHELL'S ART IN THE EARLY FIFTIES: 1950-1956

"I think maybe that trip to New York in 1950 was the beginning of freeing myself, but I struggled all through the fifties to do that. In the end I was bordering more on the unreal."

Mitchell's trip to New York, her three-month sojourn at Loon Lake, and her year-long stay in the tuberculosis sanatorium were life happenings that clearly affected the development of her painting. The works that have been selected from this period indicate her continued experimentation with styles, but they also begin to establish an important groundwork for painting that she would do later.

One remarkable feature of Mitchell's earlier work is the periodic appearance of a painting that seems to be a foreshadowing of an idea that she explores more fully at a later stage. It is as if she stores and records visual ideas until she has reached a point in her development at which she is ready to use them.

Shore Birds (1952) is one of a number that were inspired by birds on the shore of Sylvan Lake in Central Alberta. Their fragile delicacy and Oriental flavor, which had been described as being reminiscent of Paul Klee[5] appear again ten years later in Mitchell's series on grasses.

Clowns (1952) is quite a different kind of painting, but the mask-like faces seem to present a starting point for a number of paintings of figures that developed from the grass series.

Although the title of *The Kitchen Maid, Dining Room Maid, and Upstairs Maid* (1952) did not come until a long time after this work was completed, the original intention in this painting was to portray three maids. Mitchell believes it was derived from her memories as a hotel chambermaid. Yet, looking at it now for the first time in many years, she notes a distinct similarity with *Clowns.* "I can see now that the faces of the maids and the faces of the clowns are very much alike," she observes. "I can't tell you very much about it. I don't know why. Perhaps they were all me in a way. The maid on the left has red hair, but my hair was a darker red than that."

Although it was painted in the same year, *Lunch Time at the Fish Packers* (1952) seems to be more reminiscent of *Early Calgary,* painted five years earlier, in terms of the freedom of its approach. Mitchell sketched it from a vantage point that looked down upon a fish packing plant just below Hastings Street in Vancouver when the workers came outside for their lunch break.

At the same time, Mitchell was producing paintings of quite a different nature, paintings that have since been described as expressions of "the physical strength and emotive power of the environment."[6] *Celestial Night* (1954), which Mitchell describes as having "an Emily Carr feel about it," is an example of these works. It was the direct result of Mitchell's time at Loon Lake, and is now in the permanent collection of the National Gallery of Canada.

The unplanned appearance of the three cats in *Cats On The Prowl* (1954) was an incident that, in retrospect, heralded Mitchell's increasing use of the unconscious in her painting. The fact that the pattern in the sky seems to be a swirl of cat prints is something that she had never noticed until it was drawn to her attention more than thirty-five years later. "I remember that I started out painting the houses, and the cats just turned up," she observed. "I can see by the brush strokes that this painting was very free. Things were just happening. That's how I work now."

Mitchell has often described the clouds of birds that began to occupy the skies of her paintings during the seventies as symbols of her unconscious imagination. It is, therefore, very tempting to inject special significance into the fact that the child portrayed in *My Bird* (1955) is cradling a white bird in her arms with great gentleness and protectiveness. Was the painting an unconscious expression of her wish to nurture and encourage her own imagination? Although Mitchell refuses to psychoanalyze her work in that way, she concedes that it may indeed be a valid observation.

The sketches for *Street Scene With Children* (1956) were done in Vancouver but the date of the painting indicates that it must have been among those that Mitchell completed while she was in the tuberculosis sanatorium. Again, its juxtaposition of buildings and figures establishes an approach that Mitchell explores over and over again in the years to come.

NOTES

1. Excerpts from a letter written in January, 1950, by Mitchell to the staff in the Calgary office of the Income Tax Department, taken from *The Janet Mitchell Papers,* in the archives of the Glenbow-Alberta Institute, Calgary.

"Shall tell you a little about my holiday. It was wonderful. I don't think any other city could offer more to the artist than New York.

"I arrived at Grand Central Station at 7:15 in the evening, and that in itself was quite a thrill. I was then whisked away to a French cafe for dinner of frog legs and other queer food. We then went for a drive and got the impact of New York at night. Broadway was much gayer and gaudier to the point of vulgarity than I ever imagined.

"From then on it was a continual rushing here and there, trying to pack everything into two weeks. Each day I toured gallery after gallery, and saw some excellent stuff, including three very outstanding exhibitions, Vincent van Gogh, Paul Klee, and Joan Miro. These shows all came from Europe. The Paul Klee show was at the Museum of Modern Art . . . the building itself is the finest I had ever seen. Several times I went to the Metropolitan Museum but found it so unwieldy. One would have to study a small section at a time to derive any knowledge, and it would take years.

"We went to plays. I did not enjoy *Kiss Me Kate* nor the *Lunts* (Alfred and wife Lynn Fontanne) in their play — all the acting was excellent but the play sloshy and sentimental. But *Death Of A Salesman* was tops. . . .

"I saw Shankar's Hindu Ballet — which to me was beyond all else in the entertainment field. That I will never forget. We attended his last performance in New York and the ovation was tremendous. He evidently is well known in the East, having had a previous engagement there. It is most unfortunate that we are unable to have entertainment of this kind in the West. The dancing and the music was exotic and sensuous and certainly more expressive than ballet dancing as we think of it.

"And I heard Leonard Pennario, concert pianist, and the symphony with Dimitri Mitropoulous conducting at Carnegie Hall. Then there was a night at the Metropolitan Opera with Bidu Sayao in the leading role in *L'Eliser d'Amore,* a light comedy opera. And that night I saw some of New York's wealth — diamonds, luxurious furs, evening gowns, top hats, chauffeurs, and expensive limousines.

"Oh! And I attended a lecture at Columbia University given by a Dr. Klineberg, a noted sociologist, on "Abnormalities in Social Structure," and I ate dinner in the university cafeteria there!

"Wall Street is a ghastly place. It is true that very little daylight enters into the narrow grim streets. Greenwich Village was wonderful and I spent considerable time at the Clay Club, Whitney Gallery, and at Sam Kramer's jewelry shop, which had the most unusual stuff — comparable with modern abstract painting. The door handle to his store is an outstretched metal hand. New York is full of queer things!"

2. J. Brooks Joyner, *M. Nicoll.* Calgary: Masters Gallery, 1979, p. 69. Nicoll also discussed automatic drawing in an interview with Joan Murray, May 24th, 1979. The transcript is available in Joan Murray's artists' files, Robert McLaughlin Gallery, Oshawa, Ontario.

3. These excerpts of letters to friends were written from Loon Lake, British Columbia, during her three-month stay.

"I am now settled in the cottage at Loon Lake. It's about nine miles from town and I have no other way of getting into town but hitchhiking, which I may add is not always too successful as far as rides are concerned, since I am reluctant to indicate that I require a ride. Unfortunately too, there is a missionary camp about a mile along the road and so the motorists, thinking probably that I am a missionary, step on the gas, not being too desirous of being 'reborn.'

"My neighbors consist of Mr. and Mrs. Crockett who live about the distance of a city block away, their white horse Nilla, and Rusty the cat. Then there is the little frog who lives in the root cellar. He and I are blinking good friends. He blinks at me and I at him. There are four ducks who live close by on the lake, and the loons whom I watch through my field glasses, the crickets, the grasshoppers, the water snakes, and the owls on the island. My neighbors are countless. It is even a greater metropolis that London or Paris.

"There are two rainbows over the lake at the moment, and the waves are flapping against the shoreline. There has been a little much-needed rain this afternoon. Unfortunately with this breeze and with the rain, the leaves are falling. It has been an exciting day. I love a storm.

"The nights are beautiful. The million stars reflect on the quiet surface of the water spreading out before my cottage. And on other nights when the moon becomes the performer, the treed hills and the island with the tall cedars provide a dark-edged border for its brilliant reflected light. I think the owls on the island and the crickets enjoy this great performance with me. But those are my only noisy neighbors at night. Maybe there are many silent ones like myself looking on.

"This is Friday evening and tomorrow is my cleanup day. I wash clothes, scrub the floor, and make the bed properly. The rest of the week only a minimum of housework is done, and so the time is spent painting, or lying outside on the air mattress acquiring more sun tan. This is the life! But dammit one just can't ignore that paycheque completely! Talking about housework, I love to wash. It is my favorite occupation. Wash everything in sight on Saturdays. I loathe ironing, so no ironing is done.

"I am batting off great numbers of paintings these days (have been listening to the ball games on the air. Can't get any other program). I shall either have to rent a warehouse to store them or burn them. Maybe the latter is most sensible. So far results are tame and controlled. However, the enthusiasm is growing each day, and I hope something a little better will come of this excellent opportunity.

"I dread the thought of going back to work. Could maybe run a trap line in the hills for the winter, sort apples in the fall, and set up a still.

"I mentioned listening to the ball games, and that reminds me to tell you that I no longer am a fan of Bartok, Debussy, and the like. Thanks to the fact that I am only able to tune in on the local small town station, I find myself singing with great gusto, "Too Old To Pass The Mustard Anymore," "The Kiss Of Fire," and a song about a guy who has to face the man who hates him on this his wedding day. Oh, and one about a bird who is walking somewhere — I've forgotten where at the moment. To think what I have been missing all these years!

"Every second Sunday there is church service in the local community hall a mile and a half away. Last Sunday there were only three others besides myself, so it is a very personal service although carried out quite formally. The preacher sings a solo for his small congregation, and one lady plays an old organ. The sun peers through the cedars and the window, and gives jagged patterns to the floor which the night before would bear the strain of dancing feet. The frog who lives under the hall accompanies the pastor in the reading of the gospel. In the corner, the wood crackles in the stove and warms the hall.

"There is silence creeping around the lake now. My wild friends are leaving for the winter. Today is a grey day, and the hills, the island, and the lake are listening. The peace is disturbed only by the sound of the falling leaves."

4. Linda Curtis, "Artist Janet Mitchell has continued to brandish brush at sanatorium," *The Calgary Herald,* Dec. 5, 1956.

Although Mitchell was enjoying the chance to paint she wanted to be out of the sanatorium. "I'll be glad to get home," she told Linda Curtis of *The Calgary Herald,* "but I hope I can retain the feeling of peace and patience that I have acquired here. I used to rush around, going here and there, doing things that I didn't need to do. I never had time to paint when I wasn't tired. But being out here, I've had time to catch up with myself. It's a good life, really. The only thing missing is the necessary stimulus to paint — things like music, conversation with other painters, and being able to study other artists' work."

5. Beryl Rowland, "Double life led by girl artist," *The Albertan,* December 2, 1955.

6. Andrew Oko, in his introduction to the catalogue of retrospective show of Janet Mitchell work, Glenbow-Alberta Institute, March 2-April 3, 1977.

Shore Birds (1952)
watercolor, 30 x 45 cm (12 x 17.5 in)
Alberta Art Foundation collection
Photograph courtesy of Alberta Art Foundation

Clowns (1952)
oil, 66 x 76 cm (26 x 30 in)
Mr. and Mrs. W.E. Code collection
Photograph by John Dean

The Kitchen Maid, Dining Room Maid, and Upstairs Maid (1952)
oil, 35.5 x 51 cm (14 x 20 in)
Barry and Sherry Emes collection
Photograph by John Dean

Lunch Time at the Fish Packers (1952)
watercolor, 38 x 56 cm (15 x 22 in)
Masters Gallery Ltd., Calgary
Photograph by John Dean

Celestial Night (1954)
oil, 66 x 76.2 cm (26 x 30 in)
National Gallery of Canada collection
Photograph courtesy of National Gallery of Canada

Cats on the Prowl (1954)
watercolor, 35.6 x 54.5 cm (14 x 21.5 in)
Private collection
Photograph by John Dean

My Bird (1955)
watercolor, 38 x 28 cm (15 x 11 in)
Doris and Gordon Oliver collection
Photograph by John Dean

Street Scene with Children (1956)
watercolor, 35.5 x 53.3 cm (14 x 21 in)
Private collection
Photograph by John Dean

Mitchell at work, 1960

4

THE LATE FIFTIES 1956-1962

Gone into the greyed past
the happy joyous
summer sounds
silent now, but for
the falling leaves.
This is a holy moment
beside a northern lake.

JANET MITCHELL

Mitchell wrote most of her poetry when she was away on sketching trips. The poem that begins this chapter was written one October day during a solitary weekend at Crimson Lake in northern Alberta. It is the time of year when the summer residents have gone home, leaving their cottages boarded up until the winter winds and snow have again yielded to spring. Roused early in the morning by the sounds of hunters and dogs getting ready to leave their neighboring cabins for one of the last rituals of autumn, Mitchell would spend hours sitting on the wharf sketching the cottages on the other side of the lake, quietly participating in the changing season that was unfolding around her.

These solitary sketching trips, made easier when she bought her first car in 1949, became an important part of her life and work. "I guess there's something in my inner soul that likes isolation, she said. It's the same when I can't sleep. There's something nice and solitary about being up in the middle of the night. It's a special feeling." She would pack a bag, load her paints, canvases, sketchpads, and dog into her small car, and head out for a weekend of concentrated work somewhere in the mountains or in central Alberta. "On those trips, I'd paint in the mornings in the cabin, and then in the afternoon, I'd go driving. In the evening, I might do some more work."

Her favorite destination included the valley between Gull Lake and Bentley, Crimson Lake, Sylvan Lake, and Rocky Mountain House, as well as the small town of Canmore nestled on the edge of the Rocky Mountains between Calgary and Banff. "I remember once I drove out to Nanaimo with Mom and some friends. They all stayed in Vancouver and I went on over to Nanaimo and booked into a housekeeping room in an old house. I put on a stew right off the bat so I wouldn't need to cook for the rest of the week. I was only there five days, and I did in the neighborhood of fifty-six watercolors. Most of them weren't any good. Probably none of them were any good. But I knew more at the end of those few days than when I went in.

"Another time, I got overwhelmed with work at the office, so I packed my bag and I went up to Red Deer. I booked into the hotel, and I did twenty-six watercolors from Friday night until late Sunday afternoon — and I felt wonderful. They were no good either, those paintings. Maybe some of them got loose somewhere.

"I had tremendous drive. It was really something. If I hadn't been able to do that, I don't know what I would have done because it was those holidays that kept me going."

The dynamic group of artists that had, in a way, become Mitchell's family, often went off on sketching trips together. Those were rich experiences, full of hard work, camaraderie, and spirited discussions of almost everything. For example, there was the time in 1957 when Mitchell spent several weeks in a cabin, forty miles south of Jasper, owned by the Edmonton Arts Society, with two other Alberta artists, Thelma Manarey and Dorothy Barnhouse from Edmonton. The three women had a wonderful time together, painting all day and talking at night. Sometimes they would organize a gala "exhibition opening" as evening entertainment with a guest list of three. They lined the walls of the cabin with the work they had done, dressed up in sun hats and rubber gloves, and had great fun "viewing the works."

Another time, a large group, including Jim and Marion Nicoll and a number of Lethbridge artists, went to Lundbreck Falls in the Crowsnest Pass for two weeks in September. Mitchell recalls: "There was one scene that was just an ideal composition. There was a roadway, and then a creek, and then a hill going up from the creek — and at the bottom of that hill was a house. So we all stopped and got out. Well, I liked the scene from the bridge, so I sat there doing my work. Marion went across to the other side and some of the others drove on to another place.

"It was my custom to wear layers of clothes because it could be cool up in the mountains. I had shorts and a halter, and then heavy wool pants and other things. As it got warmer, I took off layers.

"That night, the landlady came in to see what we'd been doing. When she saw our work, she laughed and told us that the house we had painted had been a famous house of ill repute. So then, of course, everyone started to think about me standing on this bridge taking off my clothes during the course of the day.

"Marion said everybody going by had honked their horns. She always embellished her stories. But that was an incident I loved."

One of the members of the group on that trip was an artist named Ted Faiers, whose "day job" was working in the Lethbridge hardware. He had to leave before the others to get back to work, and his companions decided that it was indeed their sombre responsibility to drink beer with Ted at the local watering hole until midnight, when he had to catch the train home. Of course, they missed the train. They did, however, with an enormous sense of purpose, make sure that he got the one at four a.m.

In spite of the fun and *joie de vivre* that characterized these group sketching trips, the underlying mission for everyone was very serious. They were all there to work. No one was more intent and focused than Mitchell. "I remember one trip to Canmore," she told me, "I was out in the mornings and had a couple of watercolors done before anybody else was up. One day I came back expecting breakfast to be ready and I think I awakened everybody in the camp. I couldn't understand why they were wasting time. I remember that morning I did the Canmore church, a lovely little Anglican church with a really steep roof."

In 1959, Mitchell submitted three watercolors to the charity auction in Ottawa for World Refugee Year. The Honourable Lester B. Pearson and Mrs. Pearson bought one for their collection, as did a Canadian diplomat, who subsequently took it with him to postings all over the world, writing to her from each location to tell her of the positive reception her painting had received from people in each of the countries. The third painting in the auction was bought by a member of the Ottawa press gallery. The purchases were not unnoticed.

Mitchell began to receive invitations to send work to a number of important shows and art lenders' organizations in Winnipeg, Montreal, and Ottawa. In 1960, she won an award for watercolor at the Biennial Exhibition at the Winnipeg Art Gallery. She has continued to send work to the Winnipeg Show — an invitational exhibition sponsored by the Winnipeg Art Gallery — ever since that time.

The Jewish Council of Women in Ottawa, whose annual "by invitation only" exhibitions featured outstanding Canadian artists, also invited Mitchell to send work in 1960. Mitchell paintings have won several important awards in these shows over the years, and they have always sold. These events, in addition to the innovative picture rental operations established in both cities, were important steps for Mitchell's artistic career, providing her with a prestigious, well-organized showcase for her work and important exposure at a time when her work was beginning to mature. Her long history of association with the Jewish Council of Women was recognized in October, 1989, when the Canadian Hadassah-Wizo held a reception in her honor to inaugurate a scholarship at the Alberta College of Art and to install "The Janet Mitchell Scholarship" in perpetuity at the Art College in Haifa, Israel.

In May of 1960, more health problems resulted in major surgery, but by August, Mitchell had recovered enough to attend a workshop at Emma Lake in Saskatchewan where she made "a significant breakthrough." However, she did not realize it immediately. In fact, she initially felt rather discouraged by the instructor, an artist from New York by the name of Herman Cherry, whose preference for abstraction was in conflict with where Mitchell wanted to be at that time. Stubbornly resisting Cherry's emphasis, she spent her days sitting at the edge of the lake painting the grasses growing there, becoming intrigued with the patterns of their reflections in the water. Cherry encouraged her when he saw what she was producing. Mitchell recalls that he said that people would give anything to do watercolors as she was doing — pure straight watercolor in the British tradition.

"I think those grasses that I did in 1960 were a turning point because it was the beginning of the calligraphy that I used for the next couple of years. And then faces started appearing in the calligraphy, and I think it became more interesting, more imaginative. I freed myself. Up until then, I had done outdoor work — barns and grass and trees — but I think that the calligraphy was the beginning of releasing myself, of becoming free."

Mitchell continued enthusiastically. "I've always said you have to remove the inhibitions. Children don't have inhibitions. Anything goes when they're drawing or painting. Then there comes a period when they start tightening up, when they want to do things as they see them. It's very hard to knock down those barriers."

Mitchell had been struggling to find this kind of freedom for some time, ever since she had seen the work of Klee and Chagall in New York. Instinctively she realized that it was an essential prerequisite to being able to allow her inner soul into her painting. Shortly after leaving the sanatorium in 1956, she had taken a book from the library about self-analysis through automatic writing that described a method for entering a different level of consciousness through writing without conscious design, that is, by letting the words flow onto the paper without thinking about them first.[1] The technique is parallel to the kind of automatism in painting that Marion Nicoll explored.

Mitchell, however, discovered that she could more effectively approach her unconscious, or inner soul, through the door of automatic writing and spent a considerable amount of time cultivating this skill in the years that followed. Her transition into her calligraphic work was an important step towards the transposition of this skill into her paintings.

The world of the struggling artist can be a tough one, and it sometimes happens that what might ordinarily be considered to be sheer, bad luck can sometimes be beneficial. For Mitchell, 1961 was a year that vividly illustrated this point. Two of her paintings were stolen from the picture rental group in Winnipeg, and more were destroyed in a fire at Robertson Galleries Ltd. in Ottawa. What was unusual was that both organizations had insured the paintings that were under their care. Thus, in her view, 1961 was "a bountiful year" of disasters. Ironically, although she was not able to earn much money through the actual sales of her works, their destruction earned unexpected income. She took advantage of the windfall of insurance money in the fall to go back to take another look at New York. This time, she combined it with a sightseeing trip in Eastern Canada. The trip had special meaning for her.

"I loved Ottawa. It was so beautiful in autumn color. I followed the guard around a tour of Parliament and was stirred at the richness of our heritage. I sat with humbleness in the House of Commons and listened to a debate on whether or not a northern railway should be built, and in the Senate they discussed a bill concerning money for athletes.

"I stayed at the Lord Elgin Hotel, which was next door to the National Gallery. This, of course, was an ideal neighbor, and I ran in and out most frequently, even enjoying tea break with the staff. There is a fine cafe on the top floor which has a grand view of the city."

The city of Quebec impressed her as well. "The place is more unusual and unique than any city in Canada. It is a wonderful, unbelievable place — a place of our early Canadian history. I walked the Plains of Abraham, the high hill of the Citadel, and round and about, up and down the streets, rode the sideway elevator from upper town to lower town, and crossed the St. Lawrence on the Levis ferry. I steeped myself in all its pride and glory."

She was enchanted with the Gaspé Peninsula and its wonderful small French Canadian villages, where there were bake ovens along the road, two-seater swings in front of every house, red maples, the wide St. Lawrence, children neatly dressed carrying their book bags to school, whole villages of weavers and carvers, old stone churches, covered bridges — and after the St. Lawrence, the Baie de Chaleur. "Even the name is beautiful to sound," she observed.

She spent five days in New York. "Having been there before, I knew exactly what I wanted to see — the Cloisters, a place with wonderful medieval art away up in Manhatten, and the Planetarium. In this day and age of thoughts of interplanetary flight, the latter is of such great interest. I saw a very fine exhibition of Chinese art from Formosa at the Metropolitan Museum and an abstract expressionist show at the only Frank Lloyd Wright building in New York — the Guggenheim Museum. I also visited an exhibition of collages and assemblages which included works of Picasso and other artistic giants of this century at the Museum of Modern Art. And I saw the Canadian Stratford Opera Guild in the *Pirates of Penzance* in their New York presentation.

"From New York, I took a train to Toronto and spent a couple of days there. I visited more galleries including the permanent Oriental exhibit at the Ontario Museum of Art. This collection is supposed to be one of the finest in North America. I then flew to Winnipeg, where I stayed for two more days before coming home. In Winnipeg, with the clarity and tang of the air, I knew that here was the beginning of Western Canada, and the next stop would be home."[2]

Increasingly, Mitchell did not have to rely on disasters to make money from her paintings. They were slowly beginning to sell. She was now able to consider joining the thin ranks of full-time painters in Western Canada.

It was a risky decision because her career was by no means well established and she had the responsibility of paying the mortgage and supporting herself and her eighty-seven-year-old stepmother whose only source of income was the old age pension. But in 1962, after more than thirty years of learning her art and twenty-two years with the Income Tax Department, Mitchell took the gamble. She quit work. When she closed the door to the office behind her for the last time, she was overwhelmed with an enormous sense of freedom.

MITCHELL'S ART FROM 1956 TO 1962

"I think I became more confident about my work while I was in the sanatorium and it showed. My watercolors were more imaginative. When I could work in oils again, I began moving more towards the abstract. It wasn't a planned thing. It just happened. And then after Emma Lake, the paintings of grasses began. That was a very important stage for me."

The subject of *Indian Woman in the Baker Sanatorium* (1956) was a lonely, frightened woman who had been forced to leave her family in the Northwest Territories to receive treatment for her tuberculosis in a far-away place where she couldn't even speak the language. Mitchell soon befriended her. The quiet patience emanating from the two figures in the painting is a reflection of Mitchell's own days in the sanatorium.

Between the time that Mitchell was in the sanatorium and 1962, when she became a full-time painter, her work continued to present an interesting divergency in style and approach. However, it also began to assume a particular quality of uniqueness that would continue to develop in the coming years, a "new internalized approach augmented by a more spontaneous freedom of expression, together with a personalization of image."[3]

The Family (1956) was painted in the same year as *Indian Woman in the Baker Sanatorium* but it is a very different work. Mitchell remembers, "I think this is an interesting one when I look at it now. But I'm sure I didn't think so at the time. To me, it shows a Maxwell Bates influence — particularly that figure on the bottom left. There's a sinister, uncomfortable look about all of them. I don't know where this one came from."

It was after a holiday in Penticton, British Columbia that Mitchell painted *Evening, Southern Okanagan* (1957). Described as "magical and spellbinding,"[4] it reflects her fascination with the night with the same mystical intensity as *Celestial Night,* painted three years earlier.

Horses (1958) is, in a way, a surprising painting for Mitchell at that point in her work because she was also developing the most abstract series of paintings that she would ever do. "I remember this painting very well," she said. "I think I did it in the fields east of Sylvan Lake, where there used to be meadows between the road and lake. I suppose I was experimenting. It was more controlled again."

It was also at about this time that she began a series of abstracts using calligraphy and watercolor washes to which she would later refer as "The Effects of a Procession" series, the title referring to a procession of thought or development of ideas. *A City* (1960) is a late example of these works.

A newspaper review of a 1959 exhibition of forty oils and watercolors in the show placed her "well within the mainstream of abstract to non-objective art now dominant in most of the Western World's metropolitan galleries," describing her most recent work as "essentially personal and poetic essays in the abstract."[5] What Mitchell remembers most about that show, however, is that she accidentally ran over two of the paintings with her car.

Old District (1960) was painted during a trip to Penticton, British Columbia. The round faces of the children presage the figures that began to appear in Mitchell paintings several years later in the same way that the crows in *Mainstreet, Cochrane* (1960) seem to introduce the birds and animals that crowd the streets of many later works.

Mitchell's series of paintings of grasses, such as *Grasses* (1962), began with her workshop at Emma Lake in 1960. Their delicacy and Oriental flavor are reminiscent of *Shore Birds,* painted eight years before, but their significance as a milestone in Mitchell's work is much greater. "A person's life is a steady progression of accumulating knowledge — visual knowledge and all other kinds," she told me. "One day, along the roadside, grasses became important to me. I was sitting on the wharf at Emma Lake looking at all the grasses sticking up through the water, and they intrigued me. The grasses had been there all the time, but all of a sudden, they meant something. I painted them for a long time. I think those paintings were quite good. But I had to keep moving on, and soon I started to use the grass forms as calligraphy in the background, and then faces started to appear."

NOTES

1. One of Mitchell's first introductions to the idea of automatic writing was through a book she borrowed from the Calgary Public Library shortly before leaving the sanatorium entitled *Self-Analysis Through Automatic Writing.* Previous attention to automatic writing had focused upon "communication" with spirits from other worlds. It is likely that the book Mitchell read was the result of the increasing attention psychoanalysts were giving to the dynamics of the unconscious at that time. The library no longer has a record of the publication, but it seems reasonable to assume that it might have been published early in the fifties.

2. Excerpts from an article written by Mitchell for the newsletter of the Calgary office of the Income Tax Department in the fall of 1961. *The Janet Mitchell Papers,* in the archives of the Glenbow-Alberta Institute, Calgary.

3. Andrew Oko, Introduction to the catalogue of a retrospective show of Janet Mitchell work, Glenbow-Alberta Institute, March 2-April 3, 1977.

4. Ibid.

5. A review of an exhibition of forty Mitchell oils and watercolors at the Calgary Allied Arts Centre. "Artist's work showing here." *The Calgary Herald,* Saturday, October 24, 1959, p. 32.

Indian Woman in the Baker Sanatorium (1956)
watercolor, 53.3 x 35.5 cm (21 x 14 in)
Doris and Gordon Oliver collection
Photograph by John Dean

The Family (1956)
watercolor, 45.7 x 26.6 cm (18 x 10.5 in)
Private collection
Photograph by John Dean

Evening, Southern Okanagan (1957)
watercolor, 37.5 x 54.7 cm (14.5 x 21.5 in)
Mr. and Mrs. Edward McNally collection
Photograph by John Dean

Horses (1958)
watercolor, 35.5 x 50.8 cm (14 x 20 in)
Rachael Scott collection
Photograph by John Dean

A City (1960)
watercolor, 38 x 54.6 cm (15 x 21.5 in)
Private collection
Photograph by John Dean

Old District (1960)
watercolor, 34.2 x 44.5 cm (13.5 x 17.5 in)
Doris and Gordon Oliver collection
Photograph by John Dean

Mainstreet, Cochrane (1960)
watercolor, 37.4 x 54.5 cm (14.5 x 21.5 in)
Hazel Litzgus collection
Photograph by John Dean

Grasses (1962)
watercolor, 36 x 50.5 cm (14 x 20 in)
Private collection
Photograph by John Dean

5

FULL-TIME ARTIST 1963-1970

The dog sniffs the smells of the street
On our nightly walk
Around the block
While I look overhead at sights
of Stars in sky and northern lights.

JANET MITCHELL

Many of Mitchell's paintings are crowded with the shapes of birds and animals churning throughout the composition to create new realities, forms, and textures. Frequently, somewhere in the ordered excitement of shape and color there is the unmistakable presence of a little Scottish terrier.

The artistic reason that Scottish terriers sometimes appear in Mitchell's paintings is that she likes their shape and lines, "kind of rectangular, with their necks sticking out like a turtle's neck and their tails straight up in the air."

There are personal reasons as well. For the past twelve years, the many visitors to Mitchell's Calgary home have had to pass the critical scrutiny of her resident Scottie, who has made it clear that his opinion carries substantial weight with the mistress of the house. He is quite correct.

Mitchell cannot remember when she didn't have a dog of some kind, but since the time that she traded a painting for a dog named Joshua, her canine companions have all been Scotties. It is not difficult to understand the affinity that might develop between a dog known for its intelligence, stubbornness, and individuality, and a person such as Janet Mitchell. Haig, her dog for the past seven years, is a gruff little character with a warm heart who has his own chair in the living room and a major place in Mitchell's affections.

It was with the stubbornness of a Scottie dog that Mitchell worked her way out of the Sunday-painter category to the rarefied atmosphere of those Western Canadian artists who actually paint for a living. She was fifty years old when she reached that status, and she worked harder than ever, producing enormous quantities of work and exulting in her freedom to apply all of her energies to the most important focus of her life.

"Painting is a real discipline," she told me. "There's something internal that drives me — call it what you may — it's a driving force, whether I feel like working or not. It doesn't matter if I'm 'in the mood.' I don't wait for moods. I just do it. For sure, there are easier things to do than painting. I would say that probably applies to all creative work. I think if you're a writer, it's the same thing. You can find ten million things to do other than sit down and get busy. When I left the tax office, I would start painting at the same time that I had started work. There would be other things to do, but painting always came first."

Mitchell still feels that she's not saying what she wants to say in her work, although she admits that sometimes she's "satisfied or happy" about some aspect of it. "It never turns out the way I want it to, or the way that I think it should be. Sometimes when I see a painting after a long time, and I'm looking at it with more of a cold eye, I might approve of it. But I usually feel that I'm never quite finished.

"If I had been able to have good art school training," she continues, "I really don't think I would have gone the route I did because I have done things that are against the rules — a lot of things that I knew were against the rules. But that didn't deter me. I just went ahead and did it. I think that rules often make obstacles. I don't know if things would have been much different with early training. I had to learn through working."

As she continued to turn out new works, it soon became apparent that the Eastern Canadian artistic community was interested in what she was trying to say in her art. In 1965 she was the first Western artist to have her work selected for a Canadian Save the Children Fund Christmas card. In addition that year, The Canadian Society of Painters in Watercolour awarded a silver medal to one of her paintings at its annual exhibition in Sarnia, Ontario. She was elected to membership in that organization in 1967, a distinction that she describes as being her first "big step up" into the Canadian art world, and which she continues to regard as one of her most significant achievements.

In 1966, she was selected to be one of fifteen leading Canadian artists commissioned by The Reader's Digest of Canada to do paintings of roses for the World Fair in Montreal. Of the fifteen, eleven were chosen to be hung at Expo '67, and to be sold subsequently with the proceeds donated to the Canadian Retarded Children's Association. Although painting flowers was not her specialty, Mitchell's painting of the John F. Kennedy rose was among them.

What was perhaps even more significant was the increasing attention that her work was receiving in Western Canada. In an article written for *The Edmonton Journal,* Mitchell's old friend and fellow artist, Dorothy Barnhouse, paid tribute to her work.[1]

In spite of the momentum beginning to build up around Mitchell paintings during the sixties, Mitchell was earning only a very modest living. Even in 1968, which had been her best year, her paintings were selling for between one hundred and thirty-five dollars and five hundred dollars, providing her with an annual income of barely over three thousand dollars. "Dedication is an old-fashioned word," she commented to a newspaper reporter in 1969. "But you sure as hell have to be, in this field, or you wouldn't be in it."[2]

Nevertheless, "painting for money" would never be on Mitchell's agenda. She was interested only in continuing to inch along towards her lifetime goal, "to say the truth of things in flowing paint." It was in the sixties that she established her institution of The Burning Day. Her completed paintings were no longer of interest to her and if, in her judgment, they did not explore an idea well or move along to a new point, she discarded them. Thousands were thrown into the fire.

Some of her friends and admirers who knew of her habit of burning paintings began to keep track of her burning days and would turn up in the hope of salvaging some of them. Often they were successful because Mitchell didn't really care what happened to her rejects — she just didn't want to see them anymore. She estimates that she has sent about one half of what she has produced over the years to the fire, some of which are surreptitiously hanging on the walls in the homes of their rescuers.

Mitchell's health has always been a problem and it is difficult to say how much this influenced her work. She has been a migraine sufferer all her life. She was the two hundred and fiftieth member of the Migraine Foundation in Toronto and continues to maintain her membership today. Although she believes that she has been able to control the terrible attacks through diet, she has investigated some other interesting theories of prevention as well. One even involved the use of nitrous oxide, or "laughing gas" of the sort used by dentists to relax their patients. She reported to a friend:

"My dentist mentioned that some gas used in dental work helps migraine sufferers and said to come and try it sometime. So I did. It didn't cure the headache, but I'm going to try it out by going every ten days to see if it can just prevent them in the first place.

"I was in the chair for an hour, and the effect was like being out in limbo — no physical or emotional pain. The dentist and nurse looked in occasionally. The first time he asked how I felt, and I replied, 'I think how beautiful death could be.' I guess he couldn't believe what I had said and asked me to repeat it, which I did, and he replied, 'Don't say that,' with stress in his voice.

"I just felt that I had the power to stop my heart from beating, and the thought was so pleasant — all the anguish of living cut away. I did think, though, that the dentist no doubt would have to report why I died in the chair, so I decided I'd better hang on."[3]

During the sixties, Mitchell also investigated the use of self-hypnosis as a method to counter migraine attacks. It did not cure her of migraines although she believes it helped. But it had another distinct benefit for her. She discovered that self-hypnosis helped her to reach a different, more unconscious, level of her mind in the same way that automatic writing did. It therefore became another tool in her search for freedom in her work. "In learning self-hypnosis, you learn that there is another level of the mind. You can abandon yourself completely. I think everybody does it to a point, but they don't know they're doing it. You can have some ache or pain but you can get absolutely enthralled with conversation. Your mind comes right away from whatever is wrong with you — temporarily."

Mitchell's continuing responsibilities added stress to her frail health. She had been caring for and supporting the third wife of her foster father since John Mitchell's death, a responsibility that had become an increasing burden as Maude grew older. It was therefore something of a relief to Mitchell when Maude went into a nursing home in 1965. Without the constant worry of taking care of her at home, Mitchell could begin to think about making an extended trip to Europe, something she had always wanted to do. As always, the problem was one of finances.

At the urging of artist friends, she applied to the Canada Council for a carefully calculated sum of forty-five hundred dollars, which she felt would enable her to pay her travel costs, live overseas, and study for one year. Her application, unfortunately, coincided with Canada's centennial celebration in 1967 when the competition for grants was particularly heavy. An artist in Vancouver received a grant for his live art project that involved chopping up pianos with an ax and an enterprising individual in Victoria was given a grant to perform as a town crier. Mitchell was turned down. She never applied again because, as she explains, "that was the time that I really needed it."

Discouraged as she was concerning the prospects for her European trip, she continued to hope that it might somehow be possible. Fate lent a helping hand when Maude died in February of 1967. "She was ninety-two years old," Mitchell said. "I thought the old girl was going to live forever. She was a very strong woman and I was sure that I'd be going before she did."

Finally released from this draining responsibility, she sold her house to get the money for her own centennial project — a trip to Europe. She left in May.

She wrote home from London a few months later to let her friends know how things were going.[4] She had enrolled in the Heatherly Art School and, in addition to the art classes Mitchell studied silk screening, wood printing, and art history at the Hampstead Art Centre. After approximately nine months of classes and sightseeing, she left England to see what she could of the rest of Europe. Her tour included Madrid where she spent most of her time at the Museo del Prado; Nice where she saw the Maeght Foundation Gallery and the Matisse Museum, among others; Rome; Pompeii (to fulfill a long-time desire); and later, Venice which she described as "magnificent and unreal."

She arrived back in Canada in April, not quite one year from the time she had left, much enriched by her European classroom. One category of experiences had particular impact. "If the time comes that I cannot paint, I shall write. And the first article will be on 'Lavatories I Encountered in Europe.' 'Conversation in Lavatory Queues' might be good too!"[5]

Mitchell had several serious gall bladder attacks while she was away. She underwent major surgery not long after her return and, once again, struggled to regain her strength as quickly as possible so that she could resume painting.

Some time before leaving for England, Mitchell had shipped out all her worldly possessions, including her dog, to the interior of British Columbia where she intended to live when she returned. The marriage of her old friends, Luke and Vivian Lindoe, had recently broken up and Vivian had built herself a house on a hillside overlooking Shuswap Lake in Salmon Arm. Vivian's invitation to live and work with her there was particularly appealing to Mitchell, whose depleted economic resources plus the increase in prices that had occurred while she was away would not have gone far towards purchasing another Calgary home. Soon after her return from Europe, Mitchell arrived at Salmon Arm.

It was a beautiful piece of land surrounded by the magnificent scenery that she had always loved. It was peaceful and quiet and isolated, just the sort of place that Mitchell had always searched out for sketching. But something had changed. Perhaps it was the fact that it was a permanent, rather than a temporary, retreat; perhaps it was because Mitchell was no longer trying to escape from her job at the Income Tax Department or an aging stepmother at home. At any rate, she was miserable. "The first time I had an appointment in town, there was a snow slide in the pass and I couldn't get through," she remembers. "All traffic was stopped. So I had to come by train. The train took twelve hours. You could almost walk more quickly. A month later I had another appointment. That time, there was a mud slide. Again, I had to come by train. I realized I was farther away from civilization than I wanted to be.

"I was never so unhappy or lonely in my whole life — and I'm not given to loneliness. I like to be alone, but I like to know I can always talk to someone on the telephone if I need the contact."

Although Calgary was only three hundred and forty miles away, traveling back and forth was not so simple. The kind of isolation that Mitchell wanted was quiet and privacy in the midst of civilization, not a complete withdrawal. Within three months, she left Salmon Arm to find a place to live in Calgary again. Her problem of accommodation was solved quickly enough, but she was not very happy with the answer.

Eighty-five Capri was the address of a Calgary artist, Greg Arnold, an abstractionist whose sculpture and painting were considered by many to show enormous potential, and his mother, whom everybody called "Aunt Olga." When Janet moved back from Salmon Arm, Arnold was in the hospital suffering from terminal cancer. Their friends in the city's closely-knit art colony were concerned about Olga living alone and, aware of Mitchell's housing predicament, urged her to move in to the Arnold home. They reasoned that it would provide Mitchell with a place to live and Olga with a live-in companion. The solution seemed ideal.

What they failed to understand was the enormity of what they were asking Mitchell to do. She was fifty-six years old. It had been just slightly more than a year since she had been released from her twenty-eight year burden of supporting and caring for Maude. The last thing in the world that she needed, or wanted, was the responsibility of looking after another aging woman, even though she was genuinely fond of Olga.

The pressures, however, were too strong. It became apparent that Olga's family had no intention of looking after her and they were relying on Mitchell. Unable to shrug off the responsibility that was being thrust upon her, she sadly moved into the house. "I can't tell you how much I suffered. It was staring me right in the face. I couldn't avoid it — absolutely couldn't avoid it. That's all I'd ever done — look after people."

The strain was profound. "You know, when they talk about a woman when she becomes a widow, they say she should never sell her house or sell her things until she knows what she wants to do. This was kind of similar — because I moved in there, and it was all their things — and I just abandoned most of my stuff. I had a collection of seventy works of art that I had traded and bought. I turned them all over to the Alberta Art Foundation. I had nowhere to put them because I had all Greg's work to look after. And I think I turned them over because it seemed the die was cast. This was my lot in life, and I had to go on with it. I was really in despair."

Mitchell took over the mortgage and purchase of the house and set up her easel in Arnold's basement studio. As long as she was able, Olga carried on looking after the house just as she had done for her only son, relying on Mitchell to see to the gardening, the driving, the finances, and a myriad of other details. Once she was able to resign herself to the arrangement, the situation became more comfortable, and a genuine affection developed between the two women to the extent that Mitchell took Olga to Britain twice.

Mitchell was conscientious and she stuck it out to the bitter end, which came for Olga twelve years later, in 1980 when she was eighty-four after a lengthy, difficult illness with leukemia. Mitchell looked after her until the final year, when the number of blood transfusions she needed had increased to the point that it was necessary to transfer her into an extended care hospital.

Upon Olga's death, Mitchell became the sole occupant of the house and the sole owner of Greg Arnold's art. She continued to live there until 1987; she gave Arnold's art to the Calgary Allied Arts Foundation in 1981.

MITCHELL'S ART FROM 1963 TO 1970

"I remember Buck (Illingworth) Kerr once asking me if someone who could read Pittman shorthand would be able to make out any words in the calligraphy in my paintings. I laughed, but when I think about it, I suppose it's possible. I never did anything like that on purpose though.

"The faces that started appearing in the calligraphy were the beginning of the characters that began to happen. Then birds came into it. I had done birds before but they were more realistic — yet always with a bit of humor to them. Then cats and dogs, and cows of course, just seemed to happen, and I let them. When they turn up, I use them."

Mitchell's ability to allow her unconscious to actively participate in her work was becoming increasingly evident by the time that she left the tax office to become a full-time artist. "Many of her paintings of the sixties began to lose their more tangible relationship with the physical environment, and much of her imagery began to take on the same flavor as the calligraphy itself — owls, cats, and figures began to appear in the same automatic fashion as symbols of the inner mind."[6]

Children (1963) and *Standing By* (1964) are good examples of Mitchell paintings that combine calligraphy and figures. Yet the moods of the two paintings are quite different. Mitchell explains: "You can see the calligraphy in the background of both paintings. Actually, in *Children,* it reminds me of the cat paw marks in the painting I did ten years before, *Cats on the Prowl* (1954). The faces in *Standing By* look like the faces in *Children,* but it's a very dark, sombre painting. You wonder why they're all standing there staring out. Very spooky."

The Garden of Red Flowers (1966) is a vibrant painting that still retains a hint of calligraphy in the foreground. Mitchell believes it represents an early stage in her use of strong, opaque watercolors. When she recently saw the work for the first time in many years, she awarded it the rare distinction of her unqualified approval.

In *The Courtly Array* (1966), the calligraphy is replaced by a more decorative element between the figures. It is perhaps the beginning of the spontaneous blend of animals, figures, buildings, and spaces that eventually characterized Mitchell's painting. "This is a crazy painting," Mitchell says. "The faces are interesting — an Oriental touch again. That did seem to happen every so often. I remember Stan Parrot once said to me that he thought I must have been Chinese in my last life. That was when he saw some trees I'd painted down in the Crowsnest Pass. They just seemed to look Oriental to me and so I painted them that way."

Crowd in Spain (1968) was painted after Mitchell returned from her trip to Europe from sketches that she made while she was there. Although the buildings and the figures convey the feeling of a location in Spain, the work is still distinctively hers.

The rich, night-time colors and lively brushwork of *Owls* (1969) also earned Mitchell's approval more than twenty years later, as did *Characters on the Street* (1970), a painting of quite a different nature that represents a change of location from a spot in the real world to a place in Mitchell's mind. It is not as much a place as it is a happening.

Many of Mitchell's paintings beginning at about this time can best be described as happenings in which her unconscious mingles with reality to result in what has been described as "a manifestation of the outer life in counterpoint with the inner."[7] *People of the Street #24* (1970) is an early example with the distinctive Mitchell birds and buildings. *A Question of Cats* (1970) is another. Mitchell's retrospective observation was that this painting has "more imagination, more control, and one very evil looking cat."

NOTES

1. Dorothy Barnhouse. "Art's three rings diffuse spotlight," *The Edmonton Journal,* November 1, 1965.

"Once in a while the spotlight hits a painter who has been there for some time without our noticing and suddenly we are aware that without fanfare or flourish there is something interesting going on.

Sharp-eyed Easterners found out before her fellow Westerners that Janet Mitchell was worth watching. They described her work variously as "naive . . . escapist . . . near-primitive . . ." There is nothing primitive in her work except her way of seeing the world — with the clear and tolerant vision of childhood. There is certainly no urge to escape; rather a need to see in the human situation the underlying fantasy, the unexpected, the humor, the gaiety."

2. "Still not rich, but fire isn't where paintings go," *The Albertan,* January 25, 1969.

3. Excerpt from a letter written by Mitchell to Dorothy Dowhan circa 1961. Dateline on the letter was "Sunday evening just before the CBC television special, which I think should be good." *The Janet Mitchell Papers* in the archives of the Glenbow-Alberta Institute, Calgary.

4. Mitchell's article about her trip to London was published in *A.S.A. Highlights,* September, 1967.

"I was told before I left Calgary that I would feel more fully a Canadian over here — and I do. We are quite a different people.

"Never have I seen such complexions — even the old people! And the children and babies are a joy to look at. No wonder the mothers go about proudly pushing the great, magnificent prams, the likes of which we never see in Calgary. The pram is a framework in which to display the beautiful piece of creative art.

"The best free entertainment in London today is the display of fashions. How splendid the young people look! Handsome young men with sideburns, dressed exceedingly proper in their Edwardian clothes. And the girls — you should see them! They are stunning in their mini-mini skirts with their long, beautifully-stockinged legs. These young people provide a violent contrast to the background of ancient buildings and the restrained dress of their elders.

"I have enrolled in an art school (Heatherly Art School) near the Tate — originally the home of the Sitwells. Four hours a day I am just drawing with pencil and enjoying it, and finding the results more gratifying and the basic knowledge more valuable than I had anticipated. The school is really old-fashioned and quite out of step with the new, but the instructors are very competent . . . . I'm doing pots and jugs and things and concentrating on form. Hope to do some figure drawing too. I shall certainly keep quiet about the kind of painting I do, as I rather suspect they might throw me out on my ear! I doubt that what I'm doing now will change my painting, really, but I think it will give me more confidence.

"July 1: Today being Saturday, with no drawing classes, I left early to revisit the Courtauld Gallery — then on to a visit to the British Museum. I quickly toured the galleries, just to get a general view, then spent some time in the exhibition of three hundred years of Chinese painting. I came home late afternoon and, after dinner and a rest, found my way to the beautiful Festival Hall. There, the City of London Choir and the City of London Chamber Orchestra presented "Mass C" by Beethoven and "Nelson Mass" by Haydn. Wonderful! And the walk across the bridge at dusk — the great festival halls all brilliant in light and the Thames reflecting in the warm night. What a day it has been!"

5. Excerpt from notes compiled by Mitchell summarizing her career circa 1972. *The Janet Mitchell Papers,* in the archives of the Glenbow-Alberta Institute, Calgary.

6. Andrew Oko. Introduction to the catalogue of retrospective exhibition of Janet Mitchell work, Glenbow-Alberta Institute, March 2-April 3, 1977.

7. Ibid.

Children (1963)
watercolor, 57.5 x 77.8 cm (22.5 x 30.5 in)
Alberta Art Foundation collection
Photograph courtesy of Alberta Art Foundation

Standing By (1964)
watercolor, 53.3 x 76.2 cm (21 x 30 in)
Private collection

The Garden of Red Flowers (1966)
watercolor, 53.3 x 76.2 cm (21 x 30 in)
David Parsons collection
Photograph by John Dean

Courtly Array (1966)
oil, 78.7 x 122 cm (31 x 48 in)
Ballem, McDill, MacInnes & Eden collection
Photograph by John Dean

Crowd in Spain (1968)
watercolor, 39.7 x 52.5 cm (15.5 x 20.5 in)
Hazel Litzgus collection
Photograph by John Dean

Owls (1969)
watercolor, 53.3 x 43 cm (21 x 17 in)
Mr. and Mrs. John D. James collection
Photograph by John Dean

Characters on the Street (1970)
watercolor, 27.9 x 40.6 cm (11 x 16 in)
Mr. and Mrs. Roland Valentine collection
Photograph by John Dean

People of the Street #24 (1970)
watercolor, 56 x 77 cm (22 x 30 in)
Alberta Art Foundation collection
Photograph courtesy of Alberta Art Foundation

A Question of Cats (1970)
watercolor, 35 x 42.4 cm (13.5 x 16.5 in)
F.D. Motter collection
Photograph by John Dean

6

THE MATURE ARTIST 1970-1985

Silvery snow beneath the March sky,
Filigree of twiggy trees in winter,
Shades of brown.
The west wind blows.

JANET MITCHELL

There comes a time in the artistic process when the homework is done, the mechanics of the craft are mastered, and what remains is to ignite the magical fire of creativity that makes the ordinary extraordinary. Mitchell had been learning how to fan the flames for some time, but it was during the seventies that they began to burn brightest.

Like a mountain climber who never looks down, she worked her way from painting to painting, developing and exploring ideas from one high point to the next with feverish intensity. Completed paintings were no longer of interest to her; she was concerned only with the one she would do next.

"People sometimes say they like what I used to do better than what I'm doing now," she says. "My answer is that you can't stay still. It isn't that I have deliberately said I'm going to change. That doesn't happen. It's a kind of evolution. Whatever you're working on gives you a key to your next move. I'll admit that sometimes I get sick of what I'm doing. I get bored; yet, I have to work through it nonetheless. I discover through work. When something happens, it's exciting. It's a great experience.

"When I let go and try not to be in control, that's when things happen. It's a strange feeling. And then when I stand back and look at it, I sometimes think, 'My God! Did I do that?' I surprise myself. Then when I see a painting I haven't seen for a long time, I just can't believe I did it! It isn't that I necessarily think it's that good — just so unexpected!"

Mitchell has always been her own toughest critic. Everyone who meets her is surprised at the extraordinary modesty she shows about her own work. She resists the praise of others as well, knowing in her own mind that she has not yet finished what it is she is trying to do.

One of Mitchell's own comments provides some important insight into her work: "Each painting is a temporary conclusion about the inward life and the outward life — a summing up of what has gone before," she explains. "The gone before is the reading and thinking and hundreds and hundreds of sketches in the back alleys, hilltops, playgrounds, and parks, in the day and in the night — spring, summer, fall, and winter.

"To all of us life brings recurring tragedies. To see and say the ridiculous and absurd . . . seems to be what I desire most in my painting. I expect people to laugh with me and be happy. Theatre of the absurd appeals to me and reading humor in all its forms lightens the burden of living."[1]

Mitchell painted her way through the next fifteen years with characteristic single-mindedness and purpose. Her work was shown in galleries from east to west; it was purchased for many private and public collections; it was sent on touring exhibitions to the United States, Japan, London, Paris, and Brussels; and it continued to win important awards.

A retrospective and new works exhibition of Mitchell paintings in 1977 at the Glenbow-Alberta Institute caught the attention of Calgarians, who suddenly realized that their own Janet Mitchell was, indeed, an important artist. [2]

In the same year as the hanging of her retrospective show, Mitchell was elected to the membership of the Royal Canadian Academy. In 1985 she was invited to a dinner at the Arts and Letters Club in Toronto held by the Canadian Society of Painters in Watercolour, where she was presented with an award for achieving highest honors in previous years as recognized by the Society.

And she traveled. Between 1970 and 1985 there were several more trips to England and to Eastern Canada, including the Maritimes, as well as a Caribbean cruise which was not her "cup of tea," plus a tour of Greece, a visit to the east coast of Spain, and another to Japan, something she very much enjoyed.

Olga's death in 1980 released Mitchell once and for all from the web of duties and responsibilities placed on her by others. Finally she was given the privilege of privacy and control over her own life. She was sixty-eight years old. She has guarded this luxury ferociously ever since, although she has at the same time, become well-known among her friends for her consistent generosity. She spent years helping her old friend and mentor Marion Nicoll during her long illness with arthritis; when Nicoll died, Mitchell became guardian for Jim Nicoll and later acted as executor of his estate. She has made time for friends and acquaintances who have come to her for financial advice. She has contributed hundreds of paintings to a wide variety of charitable causes, and she has been an active participant in the artistic life of Alberta as an art juror, as a board member of artistic organizations, and as a mentor to young artists. She even gave a talk to fourth-year students at the Alberta College of Art on the subject of income tax, "should they ever happen to earn an income."

Mitchell's own income was not large. Even at the time of her Glenbow retrospective show in 1977, she was still some distance away from earning a comfortable living from her art. Furthermore, getting her work into the marketplace was an expensive, time-consuming chore that had unrewarding results.

Her paintings, mostly unframed, were hidden away in the backrooms of dealers across the country. Many dealers required the artist to pay for all, or a portion, of the cost of a show, including advertising, entertainment, and framing. In Alberta, her work was seldom hung on the walls of galleries for people to see. Paintings were taken on consignment; payment for works sold would often take months to reach her; and many paintings simply disappeared, never to be seen again. In short, her experience with art dealers had been, with a few notable exceptions, so negative that she generally distrusted them all.

Sometime in the mid-seventies, a former Vancouver art dealer, Peter Ohler, opened a small gallery in Calgary — Masters Gallery. Ohler, who had been the quarterback of the 1963 B.C. Lions Grey Cup football team, immediately began to apply his diverse talents and interests to the task of building up his gallery with the work of good, local artists. He had seen a picture of one of Mitchell's paintings in a National Gallery catalogue (*Moon Over Mountain Village,* 1954) and had noted that the artist was from Calgary. When her name came up again in the art catalogues crossing his Calgary desk, he thumbed through the telephone book to see if she was listed. To his surprise she was. He called her immediately and, to his amazement, learned that she had no particular connections with any galleries in the area.

The initial conversations were predictably awkward. Ohler didn't want to seem too "pushy," and Mitchell was skeptical. An appointment was finally made and Ohler went to her home to see her work.[3]

On that first visit, Ohler bought everything Mitchell had. She was impressed. This initial transaction marked the beginning of a long, close relationship with Masters Gallery Ltd. that continues today with the new head of the gallery, Rod Green. The association has, in many ways, changed her life by providing her with a dynamic showcase for her work as well as invaluable assistance with the myriad of details associated with being an artist.

In the spring of 1988, Mitchell was presented with an Honorary Doctor of Laws degree from the University of Calgary. Her keynote speech, which she delivered with her head barely reaching over the podium, gives some interesting information about her philosophy of life. She advised young people, no matter what their chosen career, to take time to enjoy simple things and also to escape from time to time from their workday existence to pursue something that will refresh them in spirit. For Mitchell, life's special moments are her riches. They are valued as precious memories which continually give joy to her life.[4]

MITCHELL'S ART FROM 1970 TO 1985

"As far as I was concerned, the seventies was a great period for me. I did a tremendous amount of work, both acrylics and watercolors. I think I did a lot of good watercolors. It was more of a releasing of myself. The paintings became much more free."

Selecting a small number of paintings to illustrate Mitchell's art during this fifteen-year period is like trying to sample everything in a candy store with only twenty-five cents. She produced an enormous quantity of extraordinary work that not only won the approval of critics across Canada, but also caught the eyes and captured the hearts of people from all walks of life. A widely used quotation from *Arts West* said that "Mitchell's works seem to appeal to those who have laughed with the most abandon and who have cried from the deepest hurt. Deeply emotional, the works exist on several levels, so that the child, the novice collector, the professional connoisseur, and artist can all discover a personal awareness."[5]

What is immediately apparent from a survey of Mitchell paintings of this time is that there are three general categories of works. The first is firmly anchored to the real world; the second combines views of the real world with views of an internal world of the mind; and the third almost abandons the real world to the powers of the Mitchell unconscious.

Paintings in the first category, which are executed with great skill, depict identifiable places and have an architectural, historical quality to them. At the same time, however, they offer far more than an exercise in strict, visual interpretation. They are full of character, charm, and distinctive Mitchell touches.

Examples of these paintings include *Road Down to the Lake* (circa 1982), whose subject is the main street of Sylvan Lake in central Alberta; *North Hill, Calgary* (1982); *Eau Claire* (1983); *The Top of the 14th Street Hill* (1983); *My Favorite Time of Day* (circa 1983). The latter paintings were all sketched at some of Mitchell's favorite spots in Calgary.

Quite often, Mitchell paintings combine a real-life location with a Mitchell scenario, such as *Sunday Skaters* (circa 1982), with its colorful, dynamic figures set against the skyline of Calgary's downtown area, *Street Carnival,* (1981), *New in Town* (1984), an imaginary street lined with real buildings from Mitchell's sketchbooks.

She keeps returning to these kinds of paintings as a way of retaining control over the fundamentals, a kind of anchor on reality for her unconscious mind. It is only when control of technique and execution are completely automatic that she can allow herself to be free enough to let her unconscious take over.

The necessity for this balance between control and freedom is well illustrated in Mitchell paintings that seem to combine elements of the external world with her own internal reality, paintings which have been described as creating "a marriage between the fantasy and spontaneity of the inner life and the emotional impact of the external environment."[6] *Big Town* (1975), whose real-life location is Front Street in Toronto, is one example. Others are *Moon Birds* (1973), *How Long Has This Been Going On?* (circa 1982), *Coffee Night in Canada* (1974), *Crowded City* (1975), *Yahoo* (1976), *Birds and Cats Keep Time* (1975), and *Downtown in a Small Town* (1978).

Some of Mitchell's acrylics from this period use a whiting-out technique that accentuates the blend of the internal with the external through shapes and colors that are interlocked with areas of white. The effect is powerful and striking.

In *Barnyard Characters* (1978), for example, the animals are both background and foreground. The fun of it all prompted one critic to observe that "the cows are recognizable with amusing personalities (each one different as in real life), yet their white patterns are the same as the background, giving the impression of holes. Holey cows?"[7] Other examples of this energetic use of white are *Love Your Neighbor* (1974) and *Market Day* (1981).

There is one more classification of paintings to consider in this arbitrary survey of Mitchell's work after 1970: those which seem to come entirely from what she calls her "inner soul." These works do not have an obvious anchor in the world outside; they seem to be solely the products of the Mitchell imagination, perhaps illustrating what she has often called "complete release and freedom." Three such paintings are *It All Happened in the Barn* (1971), with its flurry of cows, buildings, and birds; *Bird Dog* (1972); and *Scavenger Hunters* (circa 1982), with human and animal figures floating on a watercolor wash. Other examples of the unconscious at work can be seen in the ominous owls of *A View of Night* (1977), the ordered confusion of *Proportional Representation* (1973), and the potent symbolism of *Bird in the Hand* (n/d).

The ultimate effect of seeing a number of Mitchell works is the impression of some insightful, grand design, the feeling that here is a vision of the world that holds the key to a greater truth and understanding of life itself. As one critic observed, "the world may go mad and fall to pieces around us, our deeds failing to match our aspirations, but with the help of such buoyant insight as Janet Mitchell projects, we may make it yet."[8]

Mitchell, however, firmly resists any attempts to inject anything as lofty as "buoyant insight" into her work. "I just paint," she insists. "Others can see what they want."

NOTES

1. *AA Magazine,* 40 (2), 1969, p. 2.

2. Carol Hogg. A review of a retrospective and new works exhibition of Mitchell paintings at the Glenbow-Alberta Institute, Calgary. *The Calgary Herald,* March 18, 1977.

"... Largely self-taught, she paints in a happily abandoned manner, mixing fantasy with reality, frequently using brilliant colors.

"... her most recent pieces, some elaborated with watercolors — especially the sophisticated acrylic paintings she created just last year — clearly elevate her into the ranks of artists who have developed a distinctive and meaningful way of viewing the world."

3. Peter Ohler interview, November 7, 1989.

"I was absolutely stunned at what I saw, because I wasn't expecting ... well, I wasn't expecting what I saw. I think I was expecting flowers and little mountain scenes and stooks and trees. What I saw instead were unbelievably powerful, colorful, knock-em-dead interpretations of those things that came truly from the depth of her imagination and character rather than from a literal translation of what she saw around her. I was absolutely stunned. I knew right away that she was a really important painter. It was very exciting for me."

4. Dr. Janet Mitchell's acceptance speech for the degree Honorary Doctor of Laws.

"I think I have a good imagination and a sense of humor; they say it shows in my paintings. Had I pushed consciously or unconsciously these two characteristics, I could never have imagined standing in this place today to speak to a gathering of scholarly people. But here I am, and I trust that I can say something worthwhile.

"Many subjects have been turned over in my mind, but I finally decided to talk about 'taking time to smell the roses,' while still making good use of all available time in your life.

"I say, in your chosen career, take time to enjoy simple things. Who knows, it may lead to another career which you may or may not need in later life. I could name several artist friends who worked for a long time for a salary in order to provide food and lodgings, and used their free time to pursue another career. One such person I will mention is John Snow, who received an Honorary Doctorate from this university some time ago. He worked in a bank and served in the Armed Forces, using his spare time for painting, sculpture, and printmaking.

"I, too, worked in places quite foreign to the art world, but my evenings, weekends, and vacation were used for the arts. At times, I felt overwhelmed by the demands of the work place and would 'escape' for a weekend. One time that comes to mind, I boarded a bus on a Friday evening with my watercolor materials to check into a hotel in Red Deer. I returned on the Sunday evening, having done twenty-six watercolors! Most of them were bad, but I knew more about the handling of the medium, and about myself.

"There was a time when tuberculosis kept me in bed in the sanatorium for ten months. For a while, painting was forbidden, but nonetheless, it became a profitable time. Many books of the classics were read. Because I was mainly confined to one room, my observation of things close at hand became intensified. The clothing that visitors wore was well-scrutinized, since it was always a pleasant contrast to the daily life of uniforms. The pattern of sunlight and shadow in my room changing from morning until evening, and from spring into summer and winter, the opening of flowers from buds at my bedside table. Through the open window, the scream of gulls by the river, and across the river in the park, the joyous summer sounds of the picnickers.

"In time, life resumed its normal course of working in the office and painting in the evenings and on weekends, but I always made time to enjoy the sights and sounds of this city.

"I will tell you of a few precious places that I enjoy. At the west end of Confederation Park . . . , the City Parks Department has left an area of natural growth in an otherwise well-groomed park. There is a small pond — one could call it a slough — with bullrushes and frogs that croak loudly on a warm summer evening, and killdeer that nest in the grass. A small hill rises from this pond where shrubs and flowers native to this area grow. I was there a short time ago — it was too cool for the frogs, but the hill was covered with crocus, and I know that later there will be buffalo beans and purple vetch and goldenrod.

"Not too far to the north is Nose Hill — a place one must go to view the magnificence of a Chinook arch.

"Another place, and a magical moment, is to be found on Prince's Island. One sits on a bench on the south side of the Island by the steam, facing the city. The right moment is just at the time of the setting sun, when the lights appear on the high buildings. I wait for a play to begin on the opposite bank. Ducks appear demanding food, but stop to participate in a territorial squabble. My Scottie dog threatens to enter the water, anxious to be involved in the dispute. It is now quite dark — what will the play be tonight?

"Another time down on New Street, which is on the south bank of the Bow across from St. Georges's Island, I checked on an old house that had been a good sketching subject. In the 40s, the shingles on the old house flapped in the wind, and the fir trees in the garden moaned, remembering better times when the house was young and life was full of optimism. I watched the house over the years, always wishing that I had enough money to buy and restore it. Well, one spring, a change had taken place: an architect bought the house. The outside remained the same, the verandas and dormer windows, but new shingles and a lot of paint did wonders, and I was happy to see it.

"The panorama on an early morning from Scotsman's grandstand [a hill overlooking Calgary's Stampede Grounds so named because you can see the events from a distance without paying admission to get into it — this is particularly relevant for the nightly fireworks show of the Stampede], and then Maggie Street just below. This street never quite made up its mind whether to be a front street or a back alley. Houses on one side have their front doors on the street, and on the other side facing the front doors are the rubbish cans and the garages. I have memories of one house in particular. Once while sitting sketching, I became aware of great activity — joy and jubilation — the father in the small house had just that morning returned from service overseas in the Second World War.

"Then a walk in the far west end of Bowness Park on a rainy morning in June — preferably a quiet Sunday morning when the sky is grey and the rain drips from every leaf, the perfume from the shrubs fills the air, and the stream which links the river with the lagoon drifts slowly by the walk. The words of the twenty-third Psalm come to mind.

"On my travels abroad, I remember a beautiful foggy day in London. I was in pursuit of some printmaking tools for a course I was taking. The tools were to be purchased in Bleeding Heart Lane. I enjoyed the drama of the search on such a day.

"And I remember arriving in early February in Venice, seeing the famous Piazza for the first time as the boat passed by, taking me to my lodging. Again, it was a heavy mist, and the warnings from the fog horns gave out their mournful sound. Those few days were, in my mind, a place not of this world. To add to the mystery and enchantment, I was more or less alone with my thoughts. There were no tourists — I was alone to wander in this strange place.

"Memories of a walk up the hill from the bus stop at St. Paul de Vence to see a courtyard of Giacometti sculpture and Chagall paintings such as I had never seen before. This was Maeght Foundation Gallery in France.

"In Athens on the sixth floor of a hotel looking down on a burnt-out theatre — seeing a sign not touched by the fire, advertising 'Sex Film.' Next to the theatre, an old four-storey apartment block with living quarters on the roof. Therein lived an old woman, a black cat, and a white rooster. It was the Greek Orthodox Easter holiday, so a tour took us out of the city during the holiday time. I was pleased to discover upon returning to Athens that the rooster was still there, that he had not been used for a meal at the Easter table!

"I have spoken about days of fog, and I cannot pass up the opportunity to quote James Thurber, the American humorist, who was said to sometimes enjoy a different visual experience when out for a walk down Fifth Avenue in New York. He was near-sighted and wore thick glasses, but he would leave his glasses at home. One day, he said that he saw elephants crossing at an intersection farther down the avenue. You see, there is an advantage in being short-sighted —and you can walk in a mist at any time!

"One time . . . someone taped a conversation with three friends and myself. We were reminiscing. Afterwards, we thought of the very rich lives we had led, in spite of the fact that we had been poor in worldly wealth for most of our lives.

"Relish the precious moments of your life, you will have them. Keep them filed away in your memory, and I hope that sometime you too will appreciate how rich your life has been — just from the simple moments of a time and place."

5. *Arts West,* 3 (1), 1978, p. 28.

6. Andrew Oko, Introduction to the catalogue of retrospective exhibition of Janet Mitchell work, Glenbow-Alberta Institute, March 2-April 3, 1977.

7. Jean Richards, "Color has no rules for Janet Mitchell." A review of an exhibition at Lefebvre Gallery, *The Edmonton Journal,* April 8, 1978.

8. John W. Graham, "Janet Mitchell celebration." A review of an exhibition at the Fleet Gallery, *Winnipeg Free Press,* May 24, 1972.

It All Happened in the Barn (1971)
watercolor, 53.2 x 69.5 cm (21 x 27 in)
Mr. and Mrs. R. Brinkerhoff Jr. collection
Photograph by John Dean

Bird Dog (1972)
watercolor, 53.5 x 72 cm (21 x 28 in)
Joan Murray collection
Photograph courtesy of Joan Murray

Proportional Representation (1973)
watercolor, 55.9 x 76.2 cm (22 x 30 in)
Alberta Art Foundation collection
Photograph courtesy of Alberta Art Foundation

Moon Birds (1973)
watercolor, 50.2 x 70.5 cm (19.5 x 27.5 in)
Government of Alberta collection
Photography courtesy of Alberta Culture and Multiculturalism

Coffee Night in Canada (1974)
watercolor, 45.7 x 50.8 cm (18 x 20 in)
Alberta Art Foundation collection
Photograph courtesy of Alberta Art Foundation

Love Your Neighbor (1974)
acrylic, 96.2 x 127 cm (37.5 x 50 in)
Alberta Art Foundation collection
Photograph courtesy of Alberta Art Foundation

Big Town (1975)
watercolor, 53.4 x 74 cm (21 x 29 in)
John and Peggy Armstrong collection

Crowded City (1975)
watercolor, 53.4 x 74 cm (21 x 29 in)
Private collection
Photograph by John Dean

Birds and Cats Keep Time (1975)
watercolor, 26.5 x 35 cm (10.5 x 13.5 in)
Private collection
Photograph by John Dean

Yahoo (1976)
watercolor, 53.3 x 76.2 cm (21 x 30 in)
Dr. and Mrs. D. Yadav collection
Photograph by John Dean

A View of Night (1977)
acrylic, 101.6 x 121.9 cm (40 x 48 in)
Private collection
Photograph by John Dean

Downtown in a Small Town (1978)
watercolor, 55.8 x 76.2 cm (22 x 30 in)
Mr. and Mrs. Roland Valentine collection
Photograph by John Dean

Barnyard Characters (1978)
acrylic, 101.6 x 121.9 cm (40 x 48 in)
Fenerty Robertson Fraser & Hatch collection

Street Carnival (1981)
watercolor, 55.8 x 76.2 cm (22 x 30 in)
Private collection

Market Day (1981)
acrylic, 101.6 x 121.9 cm (40 x 48 in)
Mr. and Mrs. William Langford collection
Photograph by John Dean

The Road Down to the Lake (c 1982)
watercolor, 22 x 30 cm (8.5 x 12 in)
Private collection

North Hill, Calgary (1982)
oil, 76.2 x 91.4 cm (30 x 36 in)
Private collection

Sunday Skaters (c 1982)
watercolor, 14 x 21 cm (5.5 x 8 in)
Private collection

Scavenger Hunters (c 1982)
watercolor, 13.5 x 21 cm (5.5 x 8 in)
Private collection

How Long Has This Been Going On? (c 1982)
watercolor, 20 x 29 cm (7.5 x 11 in)
Private collection

Eau Claire (1983)
oil, 91 x 91 cm (35.5 x 35.5 in)
Alberta Art Foundation collection
Photograph courtesy of Alberta Art Foundation

The Top of the 14th Street Hill (1983)
watercolor, 55.8 x 76.2 cm (22 x 30 in)
Private collection

My Favorite Time of Day (c 1983)
acrylic, 63.5 x 76.2 cm (25 x 30 in)
Mr. and Mrs. Steeves collection
Photograph by John Dean

New in Town (1984)
acrylic, 101.6 x 121.9 cm (40 x 48 in)
Macleod Dixon collection

Bird in the Hand (n/d)
watercolor, 50:5 x 40.5 cm (20 x 16 in)
Government of Alberta collection
Photograph courtesy of Alberta Culture and Multiculturalism

7

RECENT YEARS 1985-1990

The snow falls in silence
The silence of time
Day into night
Year into year.

JANET MITCHELL

The rays from the late afternoon winter sun slant into the west window of the house where Janet Mitchell lives, coming alive with rich purples, reds, and blues as they dance through glass bottles on a table. The intense sparkle of the glass creates a temporary visual reality that dominates the room with its beauty until it slides away with the setting sun, relinquishing the spotlight once again to what has been there all along.

Mitchell watches the unfolding drama of light from her customary spot in the depths of an overstuffed couch piled high with papers, books, and a giant tweezer-like contraption for picking up things that are out of reach. The juxtaposition of the clutter on the couch and the sun on the glass provides an unwitting parallel to the facts of her life in 1990: the practical problems of decreased mobility versus the artistic need to work. Two padded crutches, a walker, a wheelchair, and a substantial brace on her right leg silently indicate that dealing with both is not an easy task.

As she talks, she occasionally reaches over to one of the tables that strategically bracket the sofa to pull out a card, or a photograph, or a letter to illustrate what she is saying. A cordless telephone stands guard and the black silhouette of her little Scottish terrier is outlined in the large, comfortable armchair by the window where he is keeping an eye on the external situation. As the light fades, the entire arrangement, with Mitchell in the middle, resumes its aura of command central.

She sits at an angle, leaning back into the corner of the couch with her right leg jutting straight out in front of her across the end of a cushioned stool. Her leg was immobilized in January, 1989, after a series of operations which resulted from a knee injury almost ten years ago. Now she hopes that another operation will soon enable her to drive her car again and walk in her favorite places.

The past year has been a time of great adjustment for Mitchell as she has fought to maintain her independence. She has met her problems with intelligence, courage, humor, and a firm grip on the realities of her situation. And she continues to work because she knows with unflagging certainty that she has not yet said all that she wishes to say.

In 1989, she was again represented in the annual Toronto exhibition of the Canadian Society of Painters in Watercolour. In addition, her maquette was one of those selected for inclusion in Calgary's 17th Avenue Mural Project, an exciting undertaking to place paintings by well-known Alberta artists on the exterior walls of buildings.

In 1987, Mitchell sold the house where she had lived with Olga Arnold for so many years, bought another small bungalow on Calgary's north hill, and converted two of the three bedrooms on the main floor into a comfortable studio. The house has special significance for her because it was the first home of her own choice in all of her seventy-two years.

It's an interesting home, filled with paintings, sculpture, and ceramics of other artists. The unfired clay mask that she made in Luke Lindoe's class in the early forties is the only piece of her own work to be seen other than paintings in progress in the studio. As soon as pieces are completed, she sends them to Masters Gallery Ltd. and loses all further interest in them. Her attention is directed towards the painting that she will do next rather than those that she has finished. She derives greater pleasure from surrounding herself with the work and ideas of others.

Mitchell's appearance has changed over the years. An artist painting her would need only soft pastels to portray her light grey hair, the slight tinge of pink in her complexion, and her pale, blue eyes framed by gold, wire glasses. What would be more difficult would be to find the right colors to paint the strength and character of her face.

A well-known philosopher and psychologist of this century, Abraham Maslow, wrote extensively about the self-actualized person, a concept he developed to describe someone who has fulfilled his or her potential, who has passed through a stage of "Becoming" to enter a state of "Being."[1] There is no doubt that Janet Mitchell is such a person. Everyone who meets her is struck by the childlike freshness of her approach to life, her unpretentiousness, her modesty, her passionate interest in the world and people around her, her dedication and commitment to her work, and above all, her delightful sense of humor. These, according to Maslow's observations, are all typical characteristics of people who have reached the highest level of existence.

It is somewhat curious that Mitchell remained single and unattached during a time and in a place where it was most unusual for a woman to do so. Questions about this part of her life bring only a small smile to her lips and an inscrutable look to her eyes. The questions remain unanswered and this part of her story remains untold.

Her friends are her family and she values them highly. Many are artists but many come from other walks of life. She has often commented on how rich her life has been because of them. Although they represent a wide range of ages, interests, and occupations, what they all have in common is genuine admiration and respect for all that Mitchell is. She has a special talent for looking for, and finding, the best in people.

Lack of mobility makes it difficult for her to leave the house now, but a steady stream of visitors and telephone calls keep her in the center of things. In a way, she has become a rather efficient information gathering network by serving as a central data collection point. After one lengthy stay in the hospital, she commented that she felt like a "gold mine" of information of things her friends had told her when they had come to see her and she jokingly speculated about the possibility of starting a newsletter.

Mitchell's formal education ended at grade nine when Rose Blenman decided that it should stop. But even Rose did not have the power to curb the sharp intelligence and insatiable curiosity that led to a lifetime of learning and growth. The world has been Mitchell's classroom and, although she has not been able to travel since the onset of her knee problems, she continues to study and explore it through reading, listening, discussing, thinking, and experiencing. Her living room is often the setting of animated conversation about art, philosophy, religion, politics, and current events; her couch is full of newspapers, magazines, selected articles, and books that she reads and discusses with great enthusiasm.

She is vitally concerned with developments in the artistic community and keeps a watchful eye on the activities of the many artistic organizations with which she has some involvement. As a recognized "grande dame" of Alberta artists, she is often asked for her advice and opinion, and as an artistic pioneer in the province, she is often consulted for her historical knowledge.

She is, however, quite resistant to the artistic pedestal that people keep trying to slip under her feet. For example, although the honorary degree presented to her by the University of Calgary in 1988 granted her the privilege of placing "Doctor" in front of her name, she cannot bring herself to use it. She did order some return address stickers with the title but so far she has used only one of them. That, she admits rather sheepishly, was on a letter of complaint to Canada Post.

Mitchell is independent, self-sufficient, and exceedingly stubborn about things that matter deeply to her. When one understands the difficulties that she has overcome in her life, it is apparent that these qualities have been essential underpinnings for her development as a person as well as an artist.

One of the things about which she is most stubborn is her privacy. In previous years, some of her favorite hours were spent on solitary sketching trips to unoccupied places where she could wrap herself in a cocoon of quiet isolation to do her work. She has often spoken of the same kind of feeling if she awakens in the middle of the night when the city is sleeping, or when a heavy snowstorm muffles a day into stillness. Time alone to think, to rest, to draw, and to paint is still one of her greatest needs and joys.

"The Obstacle Philosophy" is Mitchell's view of living. It begins with the premise that life presents a neverending series of challenges. Moving through it is simply a matter of eliminating the obstacles that stand in the way of what one wishes to accomplish.

Although the basic idea of this philosophy sounds as if it might provide the elements of a good board game, it becomes more complex when you add the two ingredients that are necessary for success: drive and hard work. It is obvious from the story of Mitchell's life not only that she has knocked down some major hurdles to become the artist that she is today, but also that she has accomplished this through extraordinary drive and grinding hard work.

"When you start out in life," she told me, "you can't do anything. As you go along, you remove the obstacles in front of you so that you can develop and keep developing. You have to keep building on what you did before. It's the same with painting. I did all the things I knew I couldn't do. I mean, it was a hopeless situation for me right from the beginning. I remember a fellow telling me that he thought I'd never get anywhere. I wasted a lot of time and a lot of money on materials — and I didn't have any money to waste. But there was no way I could quit!"

Mitchell's view of her life is interesting. "I've often wondered if the need to paint is a habit-forming thing in the very beginning. Once you've formed the habit, you can't stop. You feel guilty if you do. That's the way it was for me," she said. "I don't think I really had any belief in what I was doing in that I never expected the results that I actually got. I think you just have to forge ahead because there are always going to be obstacles. The road is never clear."

Painting is Mitchell's life work. To do it you have to be strong. She explained this very clearly to a neighbor who dropped by to see how she was doing after one of her knee operations.

"Well," said the neighbor, "you'll be able to paint now that you're home. It's nice that you have something to do."

Mitchell's eyes went cold. "Do you think painting is easy work?" she asked.

The neighbor, oblivious to the warning signals in her voice, answered, "At least it's something you can do until you're stronger."

"Well, I can't," snapped Mitchell. "It takes a great deal of mental and physical energy to paint."

When Mitchell goes into her studio to work, she is like a pressure cooker on the stove. Her head is steaming with ideas but she is not certain how they will come out when she removes the lid. She has reached a level of technical expertise that allows her to focus on the creative process itself which, for her, means allowing herself to be free enough to let ideas find their way onto the paper. She finds that having the radio or television going in the background while she works helps by distracting her conscious attention from her painting.

She has done thousands of realistic sketches during the course of her career — meticulous, visual vignettes of what her eyes see in the world around her. Although these representations are light-years away from what she is ultimately trying to accomplish in her painting, they continue to be an essential part of the process. For Mitchell, sketching is a way of maintaining discipline in her work. She brings herself back to it again and again so that it will automatically remain even if she succeeds in allowing her unconscious to take over.

"What I do now," she says, "is the result of many years of work. It is the result of an accumulation of so many things — knowledge of the medium, knowledge of technique, knowledge of my own innermost thoughts and unconscious. And learning to free myself from self-imposed obstacles. If I'm able to be completely free when I work, then things start to happen."

Most of Mitchell's paintings now are in watercolor, although she is looking forward to being able to work in acrylics again when she is stronger. She works in stages on a number of them at one time, thinking about them constantly and developing them further with each session of work until, one day, they are finished. The entire process may take a few days or a few weeks, depending on her level of energy and how well things are working for her. "The act of creating a painting is an elusive thing," she says. "Sometimes everything works, I know it's working, and I'm excited about it. It makes me very happy and it stays with me for quite a few days. But other times, nothing works. That's when I feel I've hit the bottom, everything I do is hopeless, and I'm certain that I'm finished.

But I keep going and the next thing I know, I've pulled myself out of the mud and the whole thing starts again."

A "sense of rightness" is a term that Mitchell uses to describe how she knows when things are working. She believes there is some kind of intuitive feeling about the "rightness" of things that is just as important to painting as drive and talent. "A sense of rightness is knowing when something is right or not," she explained. "It's something different from technical training. For example, if you're arranging something on top of a cupboard, you have a sense of what looks right to you. Some people don't have that, even people who are trying to paint. They have talent and training, but no sense of rightness. It's right there in the beginning. It might not be universal. Someone might set up an arrangement on the cupboard which, in their judgment, is a good one. But it might not be for me. It's an intuitive, very personal feeling."

Mitchell has often spoken of an incident that first made her aware of what she has now pinpointed as a sense of rightness. Many years ago, she was looking critically at one of her own paintings with a friend, vaguely uncomfortable because she knew she had broken a basic rule in its composition with a figure that was walking out of the painting. Commenting on this to her friend, Mitchell said that she knew the composition wasn't right technically, but she also knew the figure had to stay.

"Well, let her lie where Jesus flung her," answered her friend.

To Mitchell, the answer was just right.

To artists, no matter how successful, the term "dead timber" is lethal. It means that they should stop painting because they have nothing more to say. At age seventy-seven, Janet Mitchell is particularly sensitive to the possibility that she, too, may become dead timber.

Each time she finds herself "in the mud" when her work is not going well, she wonders if she will ever again do anything new or creative. It has always been, and probably will always be, an essential part of her working process. "I don't think I can really describe the hopelessness of that feeling," she told me. "I imagine it happens in all fields. If you're an athlete, I imagine there comes a time when you know that you can never exceed the high points in your career. The same thing happens to painters. We always used to say that A.Y. Jackson never said anything new after he was fifty. But Emily Carr always moved on as she got older. I know it has been like that for me so far. But you never know what's going to happen next."

"There are times," she continued, "when I see all that exuberance in some of the paintings that I've done and I almost think I could start in again and be as reckless and abandoned."

For Janet Mitchell it is still important "to say the truth of things in flowing paint." What is Mitchell's truth? What is the truth of her work? What is it that she has been struggling so hard to do all these years?

Some people describe her work as childlike, innocent, and spontaneous; they see in it the truth of simplicity and freshness. Others focus upon the humor as a statement of the absurdity of the human condition, or they appreciate the blend of fantasy and reality that combines inner and external worlds to create a greater truth. Still others speak of the interplay of composition, shapes, forms, and textures that results in exciting, new visual experiences. All are correct, because each painting that Mitchell does is a piece of her own unique reality and, like all other realities, is subject to filtering and interpretation by the individuality of each person who experiences it.

For Mitchell, the truth of things is the reality that exists in her imagination, the thoughts of her unconscious, a picture from her inner soul. She can get to this truth only by allowing herself to be free — free from her own control as well as from all the limitations and boundaries that the rest of the world imposes upon ways of looking at things, so that each of her paintings is a true visual representation of what is going on in her subconscious mind at a given time. Although she is often surprised by what appears, her sense of rightness tells her when it is the truth.

MITCHELL'S ART FROM 1985 TO 1990

Perhaps the most obvious explanation for selecting this five-year period for particular scrutiny is that it is always interesting to see an artist's most recent work. It is particularly appropriate when that work is the end result of more than fifty years of learning and development, and when it continues to move energetically towards new ideas and variations under the mature, confident guidance of an established artist such as Janet Mitchell.

The Grocery Store Gang (1985) combines three of the signature elements of Mitchell paintings — figures, buildings, and birds. It was developed from a sketch that Mitchell remembers doing in Expo year, 1967, from the window of an old hotel on Granville Street in Vancouver.

Round and Round (circa 1985) is a vibrant, energetic midway of color and action. It is probably the largest acrylic painting that Mitchell has done. Another acrylic, *Whose Side Are You On?* (1986), once again combines figures, buildings, and birds and the use of white in typical Mitchell fashion. This one was completed for a Child Reach Christmas card.

A number of Mitchell's recent paintings are disembodied forms and figures floating on a background of pastel watercolors, each bird, animal, or figure with its own unique personality. The total effect is whimsical, light-hearted, and just plain fun. Examples of these works are *And On This Farm* (1988), and *Out and About* (1989), which were selected for the 1989 Toronto exhibition of the Canadian Society of Painters in Watercolour. *Silly Season* (1990) illustrates Mitchell's continuing knack for overlapping fantasy with reality.

The tiny luminescent figure isolated in the background of *A Place Unknown* (1990) manages to steal the spotlight from the garish figures on the center stage of the work. Mitchell identifies it as being representative of herself moving towards the end of her career. There is a space between the buildings and the ground, she explains, so that she will be able to get through. The significant symbolism and masterful execution of this piece leads one to hope most fervently that it will be some time yet, many paintings away, before the small figure in *A Place Unknown* reaches the horizon.

NOTES

1. Abraham H. Maslow, *Toward a Psychology of Being*. New York: D. Van Nostrand Company, Inc., 1962.

The Grocery Store Gang (1985)
acrylic, 91.4 x 101.6 cm (36 x 40 in)
Darrell and Shelly McKeating collection

Round and Round (c 1985)
acrylic, 101.6 x 152.4 cm (40 x 60 in)
Private collection
Photograph by John Dean

Whose Side Are You On? (1986)
acrylic, 91.4 x 101.6 cm (36 x 40 in)
Private collection

And On This Farm (1988)
acrylic, 75.7 x 91.4 cm (30 x 36 in)
Alberta Art Foundation collection
Photograph by Alberta Art Foundation

Out and About (1989)
watercolor, 60.9 x 76.2 cm (24 x 30 in)
Private collection
Photograph by John Dean

Silly Season (1990)
watercolor, 56 x 74 cm (22 x 29 in)
Masters Gallery Ltd., Calgary
Photograph by John Dean

A Place Unknown (1990)
acrylic, 101.6 x 121.9 cm (40 x 48 in)
Masters Gallery Ltd., Calgary
Photograph by John Dean

EXHIBITIONS, AWARDS, AND HONORS

1942 Banff School of Fine Arts Scholarship
1944 Represented in group show, Saskatoon Art Association
1945 Represented in group show, Manitoba Society of Artists
1946 Membership in the Alberta Society of Artists
1947-52 Paintings included in local and traveling shows
1949 One-woman show, Breithaupt Gallery, Toronto
1952 Represented in a Canadian exhibition shown in Ottawa for the visit of the Queen Mother
1955 Represented in first Biennial Exhibition of Canadian Painting, National Gallery of Canada, Ottawa
1955 Represented in Winnipeg show of artists
1956 One-woman show, Robertson Galleries Ltd., Ottawa
1956 One-woman show, Allied Arts Centre, Calgary
1960 First award, watercolor, Winnipeg show
1960 Represented in group show, Jacox Gallery, Edmonton
1960 Represented in 7th annual show, Toronto Art Gallery
1960-67 Represented in Canadian Society of Painters in Watercolour exhibition, Toronto
1960-67 Represented in National Association of Jewish Women invitational exhibition, Ottawa
1962 One-woman show, Canadian Art Gallery, Calgary
1962 Represented in First Winnipeg Biennial Winter Festival show
1963 Honorable Mention, All-Alberta show
1964 Planned Sales award and purchase medal, Canadian Society of Painters in Watercolour, Toronto
1964-65 One-woman show, western art circuit
1964 Represented in All-Alberta show
1964 Honorable mention, All-Alberta show
1965 Silver medal, Canadian Society of Painters in Watercolour exhibition
1965 One-woman show, Sobot Gallery, Toronto
1965 One-woman show, Jacox Gallery, Edmonton
1965 One-woman show, Fleet Gallery, Winnipeg
1965 Represented in 13th annual exhibition, Colour and Form Society, Hart House, University of Toronto
1965 Represented in Canadian Art Gallery show, Calgary
1966 Membership in the Canadian Society of Painters in Watercolour
1966 Two-person show, Sarnia Museum
1966 One-woman show, Art Gallery of Hamilton
1966 Commissioned by Readers Digest of Canada and Montreal Rotary Club for Expo '67 exhibition
1967 One-woman show, Bonli Gallery, Toronto
1968 Canadian Critics Choice award, Montreal
1969 One-woman show, Artlenders, Montreal
1969 Represented in invitation exhibition, House of Seagram
1969 Represented in National Association of Jewish Women invitational exhibition, Ottawa
1970 One-woman show, Fleet Gallery, Winnipeg
1972 One-woman show, Kensington Gallery, Calgary
1973 One-woman show, Calgary Galleries
1973 Represented in Alberta Society of Artists exhibition, Edmonton Art Gallery
1974 Sutton and Bell purchase award, Canadian Society of Painters in Watercolour, Toronto
1974 Included in Canadian Society of Painters in Watercolour show touring the U.S.A. and (1975) Japan
1975 Included in Alberta Art Foundation touring show to London, Paris, and Brussels
1977 Retrospective and New Works exhibition, Glenbow-Alberta Institute, Calgary
1977 Represented in Alberta Art Foundation tour to Japan
1977 25th Anniversary of Queen Elizabeth's Ascension to the Throne Award
1979 Elected to the Royal Canadian Academy
1979 Annual representation, Canadian Society of Painters in Watercolour exhibition
1979 One-woman show, Masters Gallery Ltd., Calgary
1981 One-woman show, Masters Gallery Ltd., Calgary
1983 One-woman show, Masters Gallery Ltd., Calgary
1985 100th Anniversary Award for achieving highest honors in previous years as recognized by the Canadian Society of Painters in Watercolour
1986 Represented in Canadian Society of Painters in Watercolour Diamond Jubilee show, Toronto
1986 One-woman show, Masters Gallery Ltd., Calgary
1988 Honorary Doctor of Laws degree, University of Calgary
1988 Three-person show, John Aird Gallery, Toronto
1989 "The Janet Mitchell Scholarship" established in perpetuity at the Haifa Art College, Israel, by the Canadian Hadassah-Wizo
1989 Selected for The 17th Avenue Mural Project, Calgary
1989 Annual representation, Canadian Society of Painters in Watercolour exhibition

INDEX